AF264525

The Parallel Tao Te Ching

A Comparison of English Translations

by

Larry N. Campbell

The Parallel Tao Te Ching: A Comparison of English Translations
Copyright © 2021 by Larry N. Campbell

All rights reserved. No part of this book may be reproduced or transmitted in any form or by any means without written permission from the author.

ISBN: 978-0-578-35102-5

Printed in the USA

Cover design by Venessa Cerasale

Cover photograph by Larry Campbell
Location: Antelope Canyon X in Page, AZ

Title page photograph © Welcomia/dreamstime

Publisher Permissions and Attributions

Anamchara Books

Concerning all verse translations with author heading "Breed":
Verse translations from *Jesus and Lao Tzu: Adventures with the Tao Te Ching*, by George Breed. Copyright © 2014 by Anamchara Books, a division of Harding House Publishing Service, Inc. Used by permission of Anamchara Books and George Breed.

Apocryphile Press

Concerning all verse translations with author heading "Beaulac":
Verses from *Sitting with Lao Tzu*, by Andrew Beaulac. Copyright © 2016 Andrew Beaulac. Used by permission of Apocryphile Press and Andrew Beaulac.

Concerning all verse translations with author heading "Mabry":
Verses from *Tao Te Ching: The Book of the Way and Its Power*, by John R. Mabry. Copyright © 1994 John R. Mabry. Originally published in *God as Nature Sees God*. Used by permission of Apocryphile Press and John R. Mabry.

Channel V Books, a Trademark of Channel V Media

Concerning all verse translations with author heading "Hogan":
Verses from *Getting Right with Tao: A Contemporary Spin on the Tao Te Ching*, by Ron Hogan. Copyright © 2010 by Channel V Media. Used by permission of Channel V Media and Ron Hogan.

HarperCollins

Concerning all verse translations with author heading "Bynner":
#2, 3, 12, 15, 36, 42, 46, 47, 50, 67, 70, 74 from *The Way of Life According to Lao Tzu* by Witter Bynner. Copyright © 1944 by Witter Bynner; copyright © renewed 1972 by Dorothy Chauvenet and Paul Horgan. Used by permission of HarperCollins Publishers.

Concerning all verse translations with author heading "Mitchell":
Chapters 1, 7, 10, 13, 17, 19, 22, 23, 25, 27, 28, 29, 30, 34, 38, 39, 45, 54, 55, 58, 65, 69, 72, 74 *Tao Te Ching: A New English Version* by Stephen Mitchell. Translation copyright © 1988 by Stephen Mitchell. Used by permission of HarperCollins Publishers.

Hachette Book Group
Concerning all verse translations with author heading "Martin":
Verses from *A Path and a Practice* by William Martin, copyright © 2004.
Reprinted by permission of Da Capo Lifelong, an imprint of Hachette Book
Group, Inc.

Penguin Random House
Concerning verse translations with author heading "Feng & English":
"Verse Forty-Three," "Verse Twenty-Nine," "Verse Thirty-One," "Verse Forty-
Six," "Verse Fifty-One," "Verse Sixty-Eight," and "Verse Seventy-Two" from
TAO TE CHING by Lao Tsu, translated by Gia-Fu Feng and Jane English,
translation copyright © 1972 by Gia-fu Feng and Jane English, copyright renewed
2000 by Carol Wilson and Jane English. Used by permission of Alfred A. Knopf,
an imprint of the Knopf Doubleday Publishing Group, a division of Penguin
Random House LLC. All rights reserved.

Concerning verse translations with author heading "Feng & English":
"Verse Twenty-Four," "Verse Forty-Four," "Verse Fifty-Three," "Verse
Seventy-Three," and "Verse Three" from *TAO TE CHING: WITH OVER 150
PHOTOGRAPHS BY JANE ENGLISH* by Lao Tsu, translated by Gia-fu Feng and
Jane English with Toinette Lippe, certain material copyright © 1997, 2011 by Jane
English. Copyright © 1972 by Gia-fu Feng and Jane English, copyright renewed
2000 by Jane English and Carol Wilson. Used by permission of Vintage Books, an
imprint of the Knopf Doubleday Publishing Group, a division of Penguin Random
House LLC. All rights reserved.

Penquin Random House has also asked that a link to Jane English's latest material
and information be included: eheart.com.

Concerning all verse translations with author heading "Mair [#]":
"45," "8," "12," "23," "29," "36," "41," "44," "53," "58," and "61" from *TAO TE
CHING* by Lao Tzu, translated and annotated by Victor H. Mair, translation
copyright © 1990 by Victor H. Mair. Used by permission of Bantam Books, an
imprint of Random House, a division of Penguin Random House LLC. All rights
reserved.

Taoist Living
Concerning all verse translations with author heading "Martin 2":
Verses from *Walking the Tao,* by William Martin. Copyright © 2016 by William
Martin, revised edition © 2017 by William Martin. Used by permission of Taoist
Living and William Martin.

To the memory of Bob Hubbard, wise sage, spiritual mentor,
entertainment genius, and special friend,

who I *think* would have loved this book,
and who I *know* would have told me that, whether he did or not.

You are missed, Bob.

Publisher Thanks

**Various publishers were quite supportive of this project.
Special (and heartfelt) thanks to each of the following:**

Each of the publishers below granted permissions to use requested excerpts from their authors' books without any fees.

Anamchara Books

Channel V Media

Hachette Book Group

Taoist Living

Each of these publishers owned rights to *two different* books used here, and each publisher granted permissions to use excerpts from both books for reduced fees.

Apocryphile Press

HarperCollins

Penguin Random House

Contents

Foreword by William Martin ix

Preface xi

Introduction xiii

Translations Used: Annotated Descriptions xix

Parallel Translations of Tao Te Ching 2

1	Way	28	Receptive	55	Vitality
2	Duality	29	Flow	56	Union
3	Wu-Wei	30	Overdoing	57	Living
4	Origins	31	Peace	58	Example
5	Impartial	32	Distinctions	59	Moderation
6	Mother	33	Wisdom	60	Accord
7	Eternal	34	Omnipresent	61	Yielding
8	Sustenance	35	Inexhaustible	62	Invaluable
9	Release	36	Perception	63	Attention
10	Oneness	37	Simplicity	64	Beginnings
11	Intangible	38	Virtue	65	Non-knowing
12	Internal	39	Harmony	66	Humility
13	Perspective	40	Return	67	Treasures
14	Mystery	41	Laughable	68	Non-aggression
15	Sage	42	Yin-Yang	69	Enemies
16	Stillness	43	Non-action	70	Understanding
17	Leadership	44	Contentment	71	Mind
18	Authentic	45	Perfection	72	Awe
19	Centered	46	Enough	73	Net
20	Free	47	Inner	74	Control
21	Origin	48	Mastery	75	Empowering
22	Acceptance	49	Transparent	76	Flexible
23	Natural	50	Life	77	Balance
24	Excess	51	Expression	78	Paradoxical
25	Tao	52	Senses	79	Integrity
26	Grounded	53	Sidetracked	80	Ideal
27	Open	54	Rooted	81	Nourishing

Acknowledgments 165

Further Comments 167

References 179

Author Index 181

One-Word Title Index 183

Other Translations 187

Further Suggested Reading 189

Contacting the Author....................................... 189

Other Books by the Author 191

Praise for the Author and His Books 191

About the Author 193

FOREWORD

I discovered the *Tao Te Ching* five decades ago when a martial arts teacher introduced me to the art of *Tàijí* (Tai Chi), the meditative martial practice that combines form, movement, and energy in a natural practice of health and well-being, as well as self-defense. I loved this *Tàijí* practice and remember the day my instructor came over to me with a little book in his hand. He handed it to me and said, "I want you to keep this. *Tàijí* is the physical expression of this book. It is the source of effortless movement."

I took it with me and read it cover to cover that evening. I grasped about one-tenth of what I read and was completely mystified by the rest. But every word, every phrase, somehow touched an inexpressible part of me and hinted of a wordless truth just beyond my reach. That book, the *Tao Te Ching,* has been with me for almost fifty years now. I have read dozens of translations and translated it myself several times. I have written about it, talked about it, taught it in college classes, and still it remains elusive and filled with wonder for me.

The wisdom of the *Tao Te Ching* can never be exhausted, but it must be approached with a simple mind and a willingness to let go of the conditioned thought patterns of western culture. It is a gentle book in an aggressive society. It is a quiet book in an age of noise. It is a peaceful book in the midst of hate and violence. It is a book of contentment in a world of discontent. It is about as counter-culture as a book can possibly be, yet it continues to be read in hundreds of translations around the world by millions of people who find wordless solace in its simple words. It is a short, enigmatic, and altogether lovely collection of ancient Chinese characters, presented in poetic form, that attempt the impossible— to present in words the Mystery of existence that forever eludes words and speech.

The *Tao Te Ching,* while rightfully revered throughout the millennia, has never suffered the fate of becoming a Holy Book. It makes no claim to special Divine inspiration, though it has brought inspiration to countless millions over the centuries. No one has ever fought a war in its name nor burned people at the stake for not accepting its literal meanings. It is fully human, and therein lies its power.

Scholars can discuss its authorship, its manuscript evidence, or its myriad translations without resorting to heresy trials. No one has been able to codify its message into a religion. It has not given rise to structures and priesthoods. Ordinary people simply read it in whatever translation speaks to them, muse upon the meaning of its messages, and gratefully let it be exactly what it is—a beautiful expression of wisdom and encouragement that arises from a clear understanding of "the Way the World Works."

The *Tao Te Ching* is, however, sometimes difficult to grasp. The Chinese characters have meanings that are often lost in antiquity. Each character can be translated in many different ways and given different shades of meaning. The poetry itself, as is true of all good poetry, hints and suggests rather than spells out. The reader feels the attraction of the song but is left to ponder the meaning with a sense of wonder. There comes a point, as a person continues a relationship with the Tao, that the longing for a deeper understanding arises. Just what lies behind the original words? Which translation captures, in this particular chapter, the nugget that rewards the search?

How do you write a guide to that which, by its very nature, cannot be expressed in words without misunderstanding? It requires a humble, honest, and skillful approach. Larry Campbell has given us exactly that. He has provided us with a look at the essence of the *Tao Te Ching*—at least as close as one can get to that essence while limited by the necessities of language.

He has been able to gather various translations and approaches to the *Tao Te Ching* and use them to help the reader journey deep into the practical implications of the poetry as it illuminates modern life. He has delved into a wide variety of translations and selects samples from various ones to illustrate the essential message of each poetic chapter. His love of the text and his familiarity with a wide range of translations have enabled him to bring a sense of order to the reader's exploration of the *Tao Te Ching*.

The *Tao Te Ching* can never be exhausted. Like all of life, it turns, turns, turns each time it is read and reveals something new, something unexpected. On such a journey it is helpful to have company as we explore its wonders. Larry Campbell's book is an ideal companion. It provides thoughtful and practical commentary on a variety of translations without being dense or pedantic. The next time you pick up the *Tao Te Ching* and become fascinated by a slice of poetic wisdom, open Larry's book and you will be invited to take a step or two further into the possibilities of understanding.

It is a never-ending journey. It begins with a single step. Enjoy the trip.

William Martin, author of *Walking the Tao, A Path and a Practice,*
A Sage's Guide to the Tao Te Ching, and others

PREFACE: *Why* This Book?

My own journey into the land of the Tao and the Tao Te Ching started with a little synchronicity here and there, and then developed into curiosity and beyond. On my spiritual journey, I kept running into various circumstances that revealed references to the Tao Te Ching, by Lao Tzu. Presented not as a religious text, but as *The WAY of Things* (Mitchell calls it "the classic manual on the art of living"[1]), I became intrigued and began moving past curiosity into conscious exploring. Eventually I decided to read a verse a day for a while to get a better feel.

That was well over a decade ago. Since then, I have become a regular reader. Each quarter, I start rereading a verse a day for 81 days. I began using *at least* two to three translations each time, alternating various translations each return trip, sometimes adding new translations, mixing and matching, and the like. I have used at least twelve to fifteen translations at one time or another.

As might be imagined, then, I have naturally encountered several different—indeed, widely varying—translations of this literary, metaphysical, and spiritual-but-not-religious masterpiece. I have been repeatedly reminded that translations of the Tao Te Ching are almost as varied as the proverbial pens that write them and the audiences for which they are intended. Thus, their helpfulness—or lack thereof—to an everyday reader varies greatly from translation to translation, from reader to reader, and even from reading to reading!

What would be most helpful is a resource that parallels a few translations at a time, providing the opportunity for instant comparison between renderings while simultaneously enhancing one's insights into the individual messages of each chapter and finding translations that speak to the reader. While such resources exist for the New Testament and/or Gospels, for example, I often searched for such a resource for the Tao Te Ching and could not find a book version.[2] There are some varied online *digital* resources, but they have their flaws (including the question of their legality) and further require having a digital device nearby to use them, of course.

So, the idea of compiling a resource myself began to slowly and reluctantly creep into my consciousness. (I'm not a Taoist scholar, but I figured I could *compile* translations.) Once again, I tentatively began to explore. Had I realized then some of the things such a project would entail,[3] you might not be holding this book now. But, I had begun the exploration process and established a tiny bit of momentum before that realization began, so I decided to continue the journey. I hope you will profit from the end result. I know I have greatly benefitted from just cobbling it together!

Notes

1.   Stephen Mitchell, *The Second Book of the Tao* (New York: The Penguin
     Press, 2009), xi.

2, 3. Part of the reason for the unexpected difficulty of the project may also speak
     to the rarity of such resources: Unlike biblical translations, for example,
     quoting verses from most of these translations requires publisher
     permissions. These can be cumbersome (not to mention time-consuming) to
     obtain and often require user fees as well. Further information on publishers
     and attributions in earlier sections.

INTRODUCTION

What This Book?

As you read in the preface, the book came about because of a belief that other Tao Te Ching readers might like to see a variety of translations of the book—and its verses—at one time and in one book and then profit from that.

As a result, you will find here—for each of the 81 verses of the Tao Te Ching—a collection of three different translations of that verse. Each set of three translations is chosen—more or less at-random-with-a-purpose—from a larger collection of eleven translations, involving eleven different authors (including co-authors for one book and one author with two books) and eight different publishers.

But the book has also evolved into a little more than that. Due to a variety of circumstances, which I now believe to be serendipitous, the format of the book has changed from four-translations-per-verse to the current three-translations-and-a-comments-section per verse. This has actually broadened the ways I hope the book can be helpful. Now, I can not only gather and share a variety of translations, but I can also introduce you—at least briefly—to some of the author/translators themselves along with *some* of their thoughts, elaborations, and opinions about the various verses. This will be done with a certain cost (see last section here concerning quoting), but I think it can help broaden the information base—and therefore understanding? —of each verse.

And, of course, after roughly 50 readings over many years, you will frequently get some of *my* thoughts and occasional opinions as well. I couldn't resist this, of course, even though we know I'm far from being an expert on the book. These thoughts are, after all, not intended to influence, are more or less random, and frequently reflect my own humanity more than any claims of insight. Hopefully, they will occasionally be good for something—food for thought might be my first wish—but if not, they can easily be ignored, and no one will be the wiser.

A Word (Actually Several) about the Variety of Translations

While preparing this book, I put various excerpts of it into the hands of some friends and family I thought would be sympathetic-but-truthful early readers. I was mostly seeking input on the content and feel of my own comments sections, but *invariably* their first response to me was something along the lines of, "Wow—I didn't realize the translations could vary so much!" (And this from only seeing three translations at a time!) I was somewhat struck by this collective reaction, but not surprised, of course. It was my own similar reactions that eventually manifested into this book.

So, why is that so? Why are the translations occasionally *so different* in spite of their common origin? There are several reasons, some obvious, some subtle.
The original Tao Te Ching was not a book of words as we now know them. It was a book of traditional Chinese symbols and characters, each of which had a variety of shades of meaning. In the introduction of Hogan's book (page 3), he states that it "is a product of ancient Chinese culture, written in a style that would have been perfectly transparent to someone from that period, relying on imagery and metaphors they would have instantly recognized."

While I remain unconvinced of the "perfectly transparent" and "instantly recognized" parts of that quote,[1] this one-sentence overview still remains a helpful picture, not only of the original book itself, but of its background and of the perilous situation and decisions facing modern Western translators. For, while the symbols themselves might have been highly recognizable, Lao Tzu's broader messages, to which the symbols point, have been elusive and debated since even those early times.

So, what's a translator to do, *especially* a non-Chinese (in language and/or culture) translator from centuries later, and likely from the West? In some ways, it's a typical problem for translators in general—only, in this case, the problem is on steroids!

On the one hand, translators in general obviously feel a desire (perhaps even an ethical *need*) to stay as close to the original wording (or at least its perceived intent) as possible. In this book, you'll find translations that do that.
But remembering that (a) the original wording wasn't really a *wording* (!); (b) Chinese symbols have varieties of shades of meanings; and (c) a major theme of the Tao Te Ching is that using words can mask/limit reality, with *knowing* and *expounding* often being competing ideas (see verse 56, e.g.), the situation gets instantly more complicated.

So, Tao Te Ching translators will often not try quite as hard to capture the original *words*, but seek instead to try to capture the *music* behind those words.[2] You will find some of those translations here also.

Some translators will even move toward more of a mild *paraphrase translation* of sorts. These renditions seek to speak the ageless wisdom the Tao brings to today's world and those of us who live in it. ("The true power of the TTC isn't the poetic language, but the practical wisdom" [Hogan, p. 4].)

And, of course, some translators will try to seek the best of all worlds in various combinations of the above approaches.

Not only have translators approached these dilemmas in obviously different ways (as will be evidenced herein), so, too, will/do each of us as individuals have to answer similar sorts of questions *for ourselves* as we seek effective translations—and growth—for our own purposes and our own spiritual paths. And that is a key point for this book—*and for you.*

So, What Does This Mean for You?

The best of all Tao Te Ching worlds, I hope!

I hope you will find this book a helpful resource as regards the translations, but I now hope for more. Through reading the various translations and hearing snippets from various translators, I hope you also find it a jumping-off point for further exploration on your part, based on *your own* translation preferences and how they fit into *your own* Tao path. In order to do that more effectively, you will want to know as much about yourself and your own preferences along these lines as possible. Those will change and evolve over time, of course, as the Tao Te Ching speaks to you in ways that only you will hear.

As Lao Tzu tries to point out throughout, no book or other outside source can do that for you (it can only point), and so I have certainly not even tried. My goal throughout has not been one of convincing, rather of sharing resources and providing grist for the mill along your own Way.

One of my spiritual mentors (Bob Hubbard, to whom the book is dedicated) used to tell the story of church members leaving his Sunday services in his earlier pastoring days. He said it wasn't unusual to hear, "I especially enjoyed the part of your message where you said so-and-so." He would then relate that he had never consciously intended so-and-so to be a part of his message that morning. He would grin and call it the power of God working through the sermon. He said that was part of the reason Jesus taught in parables, and I think the principle is as much at work in the Tao Te Ching, if not more so!

So, in a similar manner, I encourage you to experience the power of the Tao speaking to you through the Tao Te Ching. Indeed, listen for it. Be open to hear what it says to *you*, and learn how/when to trust it. These are difficult tasks! But, if this book can be a resource that can help expedite that hearing, feeling, and knowing, then I will be delighted.

A Dozen Loose Ends, Helpful to Note

☺ Each translation used in the text is identified by some version of the name(s) of the author or translator(s) of the book in which the specific translation appears.

See the following section, "Translations Used: Annotated Descriptions," for a list of the names used to identify the translation sources, along with the titles, publishers, and a brief description of the books.

☯ A note is needed concerning references in the "Comments" and "Further Comments" sections. Over the good-natured-but-distinct hesitations of my editor, I have been somewhat more informal with references and citations there than I would have been if those sections existed in a vacuum. In multiple places in the book, however, there are meticulous references and citations to publication and author information, *especially* for the eleven translations used in this compilation. Therefore, if one of *those* authors (or his/her work) is mentioned in a comment without further reference, you may assume that is because the reference is considered obvious and easy to find, should you wish, and that adding information again is perhaps overkill and distracting. **Nonetheless, we will err on the side of caution.** In *any* case of doubt (different commentator, different verse referenced, author not immediately named, etc.), we will provide appropriate reference and citation information. (References within the "Comments" sections are included within the text in the format Author Name [year of publication, page number]. References in all sections other than the "Comments" sections of the book are treated as endnotes, with the notes appearing at the end of each section rather than the end of the book. Details for all works referenced are included on the "References" page, p. 179.)

☯ One minor exception to the above is that we *will* provide further information for Mair's *notes*, as his numbering scheme is different. We will reference his *notes* with a labeling similar to **Mair (22.2, 109)**, which will mean "Mair's note 22.2, found on page 109."

☯ A dilemma arises when referring to notes in the Feng & English book. As mentioned in the "Annotated Descriptions" section (following these comments), the notes section in the 1989 version of this book was written by Jacob Needleman. In order to properly give credit to all parties, those notes are referred to using the notation Needleman (F&E), which should be read as "Needleman's note in Feng & English."

☯ The opportunity to go beyond translations and share some author ideas (see "What This Book?" above) leads to another unfortunate dilemma. On the one hand, I want to limit my direct quoting of authors' notes in such a way that the aggregate is well within normal "fair use" guidelines. On the other hand, I'm (painfully) aware that this necessitates my occasionally referring (without quoting) to a book the reader may not own. I don't like that, but I see no win/win solution. If you're like me, you'll be anxious to expand your collection of translations anyway, as your budget allows, but in the meantime, I apologize when you're left high and dry on a specific reference.

☯ The book is arranged so that all three translations and the accompanying comments can be seen at one time with the book opened flat. So, if a verse or a comment page is longer than its allotted space, it can cause extreme formatting problems for the entire book. In these cases, my editor and I have chosen to preserve the existing format of the verse and reduce the font size accordingly. I suspect you won't notice this much of the time, and we felt it was the smaller (and more eye-friendly!) of two publishing sins.

☯ And in that same vein, there were often extra comments or text comparisons that wouldn't fit in a verse's comment section (unless you can read 3-point font!). For this reason, there is a "Further Comments" section in the back that contains some continued thoughts. *Usually*, you will be alerted to these in the comment, but perhaps not always.

☯ Don't read too much into either the choices for particular translations for each verse *or* the number of times a given author/translator is used. The former were chosen by innumerable factors that only I (even after the fact) can vaguely sense, and which—like the Tao—not even I can completely explain rationally. The latter was decidedly affected by permission decisions (from very strict to very generous) by publishers, which in turn affected not only their own authors, but in turn, those of others as well (since the total number of verses must equal 243, or 3 x 81).

☯ Early in the process of sorting, compiling, and choosing translations, I decided to come up with a *unique* one-word title for each verse. This turned out to be *much* harder than I anticipated, but simultaneously *much* more enlightening! I eventually picked my titles, but I also ended up allowing myself up to three alternatives for these one-word choices, and have put all of them in an index on page 183. Hopefully this can be a resource. If you're ever interested in what the Tao says about fill-in-the-blank, perhaps this index will give you two to four verses which (at least one person thinks) can speak to that.

☯ Along those same lines, I decided to capitalize a verse's title when that title word appears in its own related comment. I'm aware that can be distracting (it caught me once or twice), but I continue to think that highlighting the title helps, and outweighs the minor distraction. If I chose incorrectly for your eyes, forgive me.

☯ Given (a) the various conventions for Romanization of Chinese translations (Wade-Giles, Pinyin, in particular—see the notes on p. 9 of Beaulac's book, e.g.);

(b) Chinese terms and spellings which have worked themselves directly into English (*Tao, Tao Te Ching [Dao de Jing], Lao Tzu [Laozi], wu-wei,* and more) in various forms and spellings; and (c) changing trends for both of these, translators often have difficult choices to make about which of these they will use throughout. I confess to not worrying about those choices in this compilation-style book. I have used terms with which I am and have been familiar. If there are occasional inconsistencies, I am confident you will not pull out your red marking pen, even if you notice.

☯ There is also no consistency to what numbered sections of the Tao Te Ching are called. "Chapters" and "verses" are the most common, and I've even seen them referred to as "poems." I have typically preferred "chapters," but after some internal debate, I finally settled on "verses."

Notes

1. Compare, for example, a quote by Mair (see p. xi-xii) in his preface: "In the words of the author himself, it [the *Tao Te Ching*] is supposedly 'very easy to understand,' when actually it is quite difficult to comprehend fully. Paradox is the essence of the *Tao Te Ching*, so much so that even scholars with a solid grounding in classical Chinese cannot be sure they have grasped what the Old Master is really saying in his pithy maxims."

2. In his introduction, Beaulac (p. 10) tells the story of a fortunate meeting with Red Pine, in which he (Beaulac) discussed his own battles with this very dilemma. He remembers Red Pine's answer this way, "Translation is like a dance; if you and Laozi are hearing the same melody, you will be dancing in unison even if you are on the other side of the room from each other. You don't need to stand on [his] toes in your translation." After that, Beaulac said, he was "immediately released from a wooden, word-for-word translation."

Beaulac (*Sitting with Lao Tzu* by Andrew Beaulac. Apocryphile Press, 2016.) Perhaps one of the more versatile and helpful books, not just for the translations, but for the helpful resource material, as well. For the most part, his translations tread in the same general neighborhoods as the traditional ones, but generally without the obscurity that sometimes accompanies those translations. His excellent phrasing keeps the translations fresh and readable. I like his ability to occasionally insert a helpful connecting phrase between stanzas that might otherwise seem disparate, making the overall theme of a verse more apparent and cohesive. Besides his good translations, he has an excellent collection of ancillary matter, as well. His two introductory sections are short but quite helpful, especially as regards translations, Romanization of Chinese terms, and more. He includes notes with many of the verses, and they frequently contain helpful explanations and/or insights. Finally, he follows his translation with seven extra chapters, each one excellent, and each one ostensibly focusing on a key Chinese term or concept. But they also provide an excellent window into Taoist life and lore that helps give an increased understanding of the Tao Te Ching's message(s). This post-translation material is easily one of the very best sections of its type in any of the translations of which I'm aware, whether used here or not.

Breed (*Jesus and Lao Tzu: Adventures with the Tao Te Ching* by George Breed. Anamchara Books, 2014.)
Breed's book is a delightful fictional account of the travels and adventures of Jesus, Lao Tzu, and the author, in which a fun and thought-provoking story or adventure is built around each Tao Te Ching verse. So, the translations themselves are *somewhat* secondary, and the publisher relies loosely on Legge (see below), which is in the public domain. Nevertheless, many of the modifications and re-wordings are quite good, I think, and add extra insight here and there, so I have used some of them where I might otherwise have used Legge (or others). (See verse 6 [Mother], e.g., for both Legge and Breed side-by-side.) And, as an aside, the addition of the anecdotes, conversations, and lessons accompanying the story (delivered as if from Jesus and Lao Tzu themselves!) makes the entire book an enjoyable possession.

Bynner (*The Way of Life According to Lao Tzu* by Witter Bynner. A Perigee Book published by the Berkley Publishing Group, a division of Penguin Putnam, Inc., 1986.)
As might be expected from the second oldest of these translations (original copyright 1944), it carries the more traditional—sometimes stilted—translations and wordings. But there are real gems in here, ranging from subtle wordings to

entire verses. Another strength is the lengthy introductory material on the facts and legends surrounding Lao Tzu himself.

Feng & English (*Tao Te Ching* by Lao Tsu. Translated by Gia-fu Feng and Jane English with introduction and notes by Jacob Needleman. Vintage Books, a division of Random House, Inc., 1989.)
There are two separate-but-related editions of this book. Throughout this project, I have used the older 1989 Vintage Books edition, but there is another newer (2011) —and apparently significantly different—version of the book, which needs to be noted as well. The back cover notes it is "Refreshed and revised" by Jane English and her long-time editor Toinette Lippe. It also features many beautiful black/white photographs by Jane English, *as well as* corresponding Chinese translations on each facing page. I do not know this firsthand, having only come to the book not long ago, but evidence suggests (and a cursory look seems to confirm) this newer version does, indeed, have some advantages over the old one,[1] and I'm anxious to dive into it. In my mind, however, two gigantic strengths of the older version are the introduction and the notes/comments section in the back. Both are written by Jacob Needleman, and both are among the best available, especially the notes. These are worth the price of admission alone. The introduction *is* preserved in the newer book, but *not* the comments. If it were me (and it's not!), I would want both versions, for even if the newer one has fresher translations (and beautiful photos), I would not want to give up Needleman's helpful and insightful comments in the older version.

Hogan (*Getting Right with Tao: A Contemporary Spin on the Tao Te Ching*, by Ron Hogan. Channel V Books, a division of Channel V Media, 2010.)
In a collection of unique translations (and ignoring the logical contradiction), this one may be the *most* unique! The author's goal is to render the Tao Te Ching in a voice and vernacular "that might be more easily recognizable to contemporary Americans" (introduction, p. 4), and in this he certainly succeeds, though the results are sometimes unexpected—occasionally even jarring. But they are also often refreshing—even funny—and helpful as well. I share Hogan's feeling (in his introduction, p. 6) that in verse 20, Lao Tzu did not intend to open with (the Chinese equivalent of?) "Don't spend too much time thinking about stupid shit." But that rendition speaks to me, and is one of the translations I used for that verse. I'm glad I discovered this book in time to be included in my stingy-baker's dozen of translation resources.

Legge (*Tao Te Ching* by Lao Tzu. Translated with commentary by James Legge. Digireads.com Publishing, 2016.)
When I found this translation, I had been looking for a classic, older, public domain rendition to include in my collection—for a couple of reasons, really. It's understandably traditional and sometimes even obscure, but I was pleasantly

surprised by the translation, and it continues to fascinate and surprise me. One of the reasons is its variety. Much of the time, the verses are in the traditional free verse form, but he thinks nothing of switching to rhyming at the drop of a hat, even for just one stanza of one verse. And occasionally he will even present a more prose/explanatory approach. (See verse 19 for an example of both prose and rhyme!) Another helpful feature is his frequent parenthetical additions within the verse, which clarify and add context to the translation, and these usually are very helpful. Partly because this translation is now in the public domain, you will find multiple books which contain it. I consulted a few, but I prefer the DigiReads one listed above, as it also has some of Legge's own comments (though I chose not to number the stanzas of each verse as that version does).

Mair (*TAO TE CHING* by Lao Tzu. Translated and annotated by Victor H. Mair. Bantam Books, 1990.)
For better or worse (and of course opinions will vary!), there is little question that Mair's is the most scholarly of the translations included here. He has copious notes in the back, with clearly the best historical, cultural, and etymological backgrounds of the entire group, and some of these can be quite helpful and enlightening, *especially* as they related to translation details and choices. He also has a lengthy and informative afterword section that contains a wealth of background information. **It should be noted** that Mair bases his translation on more recently (1973) discovered Ma-Wang-Tui manuscripts, and he uses that non-traditional numbering system for his verses. That can be a little inconvenient, though both numberings are made clear for each verse (and are also noted in each verse's heading in *this* book). In the translations, some of his choices for wording or phrasing are quite interesting, and while they are often wordier than most, there were times that they would reach out of the pages, grab me, shake my perceptions up, and hold me temporarily speechless (see my comment in verse 1, for example). A helpful book and translation, all around.

Mabry (*Tao Te Ching: The Book of the Way and Its Power* by John R. Mabry. Apocryphile Press, 1994.)
Regrettably, I came to this translation later than many of the others, but it has quickly moved up the ladder in terms of personal favorites. You can feel its desire to stay loyal to the original/classic interpretations, yet it remains quite readable, with fresh and insightful wordings which can be helpful to modern, especially Western, readers. There are two slightly different versions of this book, although both contain the same translations. The original version appeared as *God as Nature Sees God: A Christian Reading of the Tao Te Ching*, while the later version (mentioned above) contains the translations only.

Martin (*A Path and a Practice* by William Martin. Marlowe & Company, an imprint of Avalon Publishing Group, Inc., 2005.)
Luckily, I discovered this translation in the early stages of my Tao wanderings, and it had a huge part in drawing me further into the world of the Tao and the Tao Te Ching. For quite a while, this translation and the one of Mitchell's were the only two I used in my readings, and they formed a perfect balance for me—both quite readable, but with different wordings that simultaneously held my attention and provided enough early variety to spark my curiosity. He is less wedded to the traditional leadership/government/military themes and, instead, gently applies those verses (along with others) to our daily lives in an insightful—and often beautiful—way. It is still my go-to translation if I want to know "How does this apply to me?" Like Beaulac's, this book's usefulness extends well beyond the translations. Note the title here: *A Path and a Practice*. These are the names of the excellent sections that precede and follow, respectively, his actual set of translations. "The Practice" section contains an expanded comment (with questions) for each verse. "The Path" is an absolute *must-read!* It is the best overview of what the Tao *is* (in the form of eleven statements with comments, using excerpts of verses to highlight characteristics of "The Path") that I have seen, bar none. I often reread it carefully at the end of each quarter's readings, before the next quarter starts.

Martin 2 (*Walking the Tao* by William Martin. Taoist Living, 2016.)
This translation emerged roughly a decade after the book above. It grew out of the notes from a Martin class on the Tao Te Ching, and the publication was handled by the author himself. (See the acknowledgments for what that meant to me.) It is a slightly different format (somewhat more informal, with less ancillary material, and comments following each verse, rather than in the back), but contains the same kinds of unique insights as the first. One of the interesting parts of this book for me, having grown up on his first one, is to see how the insights and focus are *different* (not better or worse, mind you) and how his voice has changed over that decade. I never know which of his translations I'll like better on any given reading.

Mitchell (*Tao Te Ching: A New English Version* by Stephen Mitchell. Harper Perennial Modern Classics edition, HarperCollins Publishers, 2006.)
As indicated above (see Martin), I cut my Tao Te Ching teeth on the duo of this book and Martin's, and for that, I am most grateful. Mitchell is one of the most readable renditions available (and therefore one of the more popular in general). He tends to be more traditional than, say Martin, but definitely *not* overly so.[2] He will paraphrase, as he feels is needed, but will often include a more traditional rendition in his notes in the back, especially, say, in the last 30 verses or so.

Notes

1. The translations *do* appear to be somewhat fresher, and I note that Alan Cohen, in his excellent book *The Tao Made Easy* (Carlsbad, CA: Hay House, Inc., 2018), p. xv, remarks that he uses this version exclusively in his examples.

2. Indeed, Mitchell refers to his book (see p. 12 of the book's P.S. section) as a "version" rather than a "translation" for this reason.

The Parallel Tao Te Ching

1
Way

Mitchell

The tao that can be told
is not the eternal Tao.
The name that can be named
is not the eternal Name.

The unnamable is the eternally
    real.
Naming is the origin
of all particular things.

Free from desire, you realize the
    mystery.
Caught in desire, you see only
    the manifestations.

Yet mystery and manifestations
arise from the same source.
This source is called darkness.

Darkness within darkness.
The gateway to all understanding.

1
Way

Martin

Talking about a path
is not walking that path.
Thinking about life
is not living.

Directly experiencing life
brings unconditional appreciation
and unity.
Thinking about life
brings conditional judgments
and separation.

Free of conditioned thinking,
we experience our true nature.
Caught in conditioned thinking,
we experience only who we think
    we are.

Yet both our conditioned nature
and our true nature
are part of life itself.
Our conditioned experience of living
is a gateway to unconditional life.

1
Way

Mair 45

The ways that can be walked are
   not the eternal Way;
The names that can be named are
   not the eternal name.
The nameless is the origin of the
   myriad creatures;
The named is the mother of the
   myriad creatures.

Therefore,
   Always be without desire
     in order to observe its
     wondrous subtleties;
   Always have desire
     so that you may observe its
     manifestations.

   Both of these derive from the
     same source;
   They have different names but
     the same designation.

Mystery of mysteries,
The gate of all wonders!

Comments

☯ The house lights have gone down, the show is about to start, and you'll be glad you're in your seats as the curtain goes up! For here, right out of the gates, we have *the* classic verse of the Tao Te Ching. Almost anyone who has heard of the book is familiar with at least one of the seemingly 628 different ways to express the opening line.

☯ I've always found it somewhat ironic that even in this first attempt to talk about the Tao, it is highlighted by what it *is not*, rather than what it *is*. I guess this is not so ironic since it underscores what the Tao Te Ching will repeatedly stress, namely that describing the Tao is impossible! See Further Comments for more thoughts on this and the entire verse.

☯ I must have read variations of this verse (including Mair's) dozens of times before this happened. Out of the clear blue in one reading, I was suddenly stopped in my tracks by Mair's wording in the 2nd stanza (see left) about the dual nature and benefits of desire. I still find that stanza marvelous food for thought and most enlightening.

☯ I very much like how Martin sets an early tone (maintained throughout his translation) of talking about these themes in terms of our "conditioned thinking" and its relation to our "true nature."

2
Duality

Beaulac

Perceiving some things as beautiful
requires the concept of "ugly."
Perceiving some things as good
requires the concept of "bad."
Likewise,
   being and non-being require each
     other;
   difficult and easy perfect each
     other;
   long and short define each other;
   it takes tones and intervals to
     make a melody;
   front and back assume each other.

This is why the sage:
   does not force things in daily
    affairs
   and does not use words to convey
    her teaching.
   The myriad things arise though
    she doesn't begin them.
   She acts, but without
    expectations,
   achieves, but without dwelling on
    it.
The sage finds no reason to cling,
   and yet nothing is lost.

2
Duality

Martin 2

We can't speak of beauty without
   knowing ugliness.
We can't speak of virtue without
   knowing vice.
We can't speak of life without
   knowing death.
We can't achieve without knowing
   failure.
We can't find silence without
   knowing noise.
Therefore why do we strive and
   strain
to keep things in place?
Much better to enjoy our work,
with no thought of reward;
to enjoy our achievements,
with no thought of honor; and our
   life,
with no thought of clinging.

2
Duality

Bynner

People through finding something
    beautiful
Think something else unbeautiful,
Through finding one man fit
Judge another unfit.
Life and death, though stemming
    from each other, seem to conflict
    as stages of change,
Difficult and easy as phases of
    achievement,
Long and short as measures of
    contrast,
High and low as degrees of relation;
But, since the varying of tones gives
    music to a voice
And what is is the was of what shall
    be,
The sanest man
Sets up no deed,
Lays down no law,
Takes everything that happens as it
    comes,
As something to animate, not to
    appropriate,
To earn, not to own,
To accept naturally without
    self-importance:
If you never assume importance
You never lose it.

Comments

☯ "This chapter introduces the essential duality of life," begins Martin 2 in his note. To me, it also indicates how naming things actually contributes to this Duality.

☯ The first half of the verse also gives rise to the second half, which is our first introduction to the concept of *wu-wei* (do without *doing*). I think Beaulac's "This is why the sage" section does a better job of making that transition clear than some other translations do.

☯ This transition between duality and *wu-wei* reminds me (in a way that I'd never quite thought of before) that "doing without doing" is really another subtle way of expressing the duality (*do*) arising from the unity (*without doing*).

☯ I'm always struck by a thought in Mitchell's notes. Referring to the master/sage acting "without doing anything," he says, "She is like an actress who loves her role. The Tao is writing the script." See Further Comments for a similar comment from Joseph Campbell.

3
Wu-Wei

Mabry

Do not exalt people who are
    extraordinarily talented
Or the people will become
    competitive.

      Do not value precious goods
      Or the people will become
        thieves.

Do not make a public display of
    riches and finery
Or the people's hearts will be
    envious and discontent.

Therefore, the wise leader will empty
    their hearts of coveting
and fill their bellies with sustenance.
      He discourages their ambition
      and strengthens their bones.
If the people are simple and free
    from desire,
the crafty will not dare to take
    advantage of them.

By practicing "not doing," nothing
    will remain undone.

3
Wu-Wei

Feng & English

Not exalting the gifted prevents
    quarreling.
Not collecting treasures prevents
    stealing.
Not seeing desirable things prevents
    confusion of the heart.

The wise therefore rule by emptying
    hearts and stuffing bellies, by
    weakening ambitions and
    strengthening bones.
If men lack knowledge and desire,
    then clever people will not try to
    interfere.
If nothing is done, then all will be
    well.

3
Wu-Wei

Bynner

It is better not to make merit a matter
  of reward
Lest people conspire and contend,
Not to pile up rich belongings
Lest they rob,
Not to excite by display
Lest they covet.
A sound leader's aim
Is to open people's hearts,
Fill their stomachs,
Calm their wills,
Brace their bones
And so to clarify their thoughts and
  cleanse their needs
That no cunning meddler could touch
  them:
Without being forced, without strain
  or constraint,
Good government comes of itself.

Comments

☯ This verse continues the duality theme started in verse 2 but begins to broaden it to extend to wiser ways of living, as well as (in most translations) the first references to the qualities of a good leader.

☯ And in that vein, we see the notion of *Wu-Wei* revisited, in ways that apply to leadership and good government (see Bynner's last line), as well as in general (see the last lines of Mabry and Feng & English).

☯ I confess to occasional uncertainties about this verse, especially the first couple of lines. I understand the wisdom in "not exalting," but are we never to at least *recognize* the genius of say, a Shakespeare, a Da Vinci, a Marie Curie, or a Yo Yo Ma (or even a Patrick Mahomes!)? I won't ever feel *competitive* (*à la* Mabry) with any of them. Where do we draw the line?

4
Origins

Mabry

The Tao is like an empty pitcher,
Poured from, but never drained.
Infinitely deep, it is the source of all
  things.

    It blunts the sharp,
    Unties the knotted,
    Shades the bright,
    Unites with all dust.

Dimly seen, yet eternally present,
I do not know who gave birth to it,
It is older than any conception of
  God.

4
Origins

Martin 2

The universe appears as mostly
  empty space.
Yet it is filled with a hidden
and inexhaustible energy
that has existed since before the
  beginning
of beginning-less time.
So we can relax and let our tension
  drain away,
for we belong to this.

4
Origins

Hogan

How much Tao is there?
More than you'll ever need.
Use all you want,
there's plenty more where that came
    from.

You can't see Tao, but it's there.
Damned if I know where it came
    from.
It's just always been around.

Comments

☯ Some translators, including Hogan here, delete the second stanza, which often appears in wording similar to Mabry's. Mitchell, in his comments, notes that it appears to be an interpolation of similar phrasing in verse 56.

☯ Martin 2 calls this verse "one of the 'mystical' poems that calls attention to the unfathomable mystery of the Tao." (See similar thoughts in the comments in verse 72 [Awe].) He further comments that we "belong to this Mystery . . . as the cells of a tree belong to that tree; an integral part of the whole tree."

☯ I'm always intrigued by lines similar to Hogan's "Use all you want," referring to the Tao. This theme (of co-creating?) is picked up again in verse 6.

5
Impartial

Mabry

Heaven and Earth are impartial,
They allow things to die.

The Sage is not sentimental,
She knows that all beings must pass
    away.

The space between Heaven and Earth
    is like a bellows
Empty, yet inexhaustible
The more it is used, the more it
    produces.

Trying to explain it will only exhaust
    you.
It is better to hold on to paradox.

5
Impartial

Martin 2

The Tao has no preference
for one thing over another.
Everything belongs, without
    distinction.
Therefore it never tries
and is always new and fresh.
We, of course, make distinctions,
    exhausting ourselves
by preferring this, and disdaining
    that;
clinging here and avoiding there.
How sad, for we were made for quiet
    peace and joy.

5
Impartial

Hogan

Tao's neutral: It doesn't worry about
    good or evil.
The Masters are neutral: They treat
    everyone the same.

Lao Tzu said Tao is like a bellows:
It's empty, but it could help set the
    world on fire.
If you keep using Tao, it works
    better.
If you keep talking about it, it won't
    make any sense.

Be cool.

Comments

☯ Verse 5 is often called the "Straw Dogs Verse" (at least by me), due to the reference by most traditional translators to ancient ritual objects called "straw dogs," revered before and during a ceremony, then discarded afterward.

☯ There are usually sentences translated roughly as, "The Master treats all people like straw dogs." Obviously, this sounds harsh and can be confusing. Those translators who still tackle this terminology often have extended background notes on this. See Further Comments for more information.

☯ Some translators (such as the three chosen here), omit references to straw dogs at all, choosing instead to focus on the broader theme of benign impartiality ("Heaven and earth are impartial"—Mabry), which in fact does appear to be the main intent of the message.

☯ Equally as puzzling in this verse can be the image of the Tao as a "bellows, empty yet inexhaustible." I like Mabry's wording of Lao Tzu's advice, "Trying to explain it will only exhaust you. It is better to hold on to the paradox." And, Hogan's: "If you keep using Tao, it works better. If you keep talking about it, it won't make any sense."

6
Mother

Breed

The valley spirit dies not; it is always
the same.
We call it the feminine mystery.
Her gate is called the root from
which grew heaven and earth.
Long and unbroken its power
remains.
Use it with the gentlest touch.

Martin 2

Everything that is, has been, or will
be;
emerges from, is contained in,
and returns to the Tao.
This is why the Tao
is called, "Mother of All."
We don't need to search for her.
No effort is needed to find her.
She is always with us.
She is us.

6
Mother

Legge

The valley spirit dies not, aye the
    same;
The female mystery thus do we
    name.
Its gate, from which at first they
    issued forth,
Is called the root from which grew
    heaven and earth.
Long and unbroken does its power
    remain,
Used gently, and without the touch of
    pain.

Comments

☯ The "valley spirit" is one of the less direct ways the Tao Te Ching refers to the feminine principle (yin) of the Tao, which is considered the Mother of creation.

☯ In his note, Martin 2 makes an interesting point. He notes that the term Mother "implies bringing into existence by birthing, rather than by making or fashioning." He later goes on to suggest that in viewing ourselves as being birthed instead of created, it is easier to identify with emerging "from within, from the very nature of the Tao, and we remain the same 'stuff' as the Tao." (In a slightly different context, there is a remark similar to this in Mitchell's note to verse 34.)

☯ I have often heard the phrase, "We were born to be co-creators," or similar. This verse (see also verse 4) provides various hints of that sentiment, some subtle, some not. Mitchell translates the last line, "You can use it any way you want." Also, in his notes (quoting Chu Hsi): "The female is the one who receives something, *and with it creates*. This creative principle is the most marvelous thing in the universe." (Italics mine.)

Eternal

Mitchell

The Tao is infinite, eternal.
Why is it eternal?
It was never born;
thus it can never die.
Why is it infinite?
It has no desires for itself;
thus it is present for all beings.

The Master stays behind;
that is why she is ahead.
She is detached from all things;
that is why she is one with them.
Because she has let go of herself,
she is perfectly fulfilled.

Eternal

Martin

How can we find the eternal,
the lasting nature of the Tao,
that seems so elusive amid the
   changes of life?

The Tao does not come and go
as do all formations.
It is the watcher of the comings
and the goings.

In our practice we find
that we are the watcher as well.
We watch our opinions and ideas,
our likes and dislikes,
our desires and our fears,
our bodies and our minds,
but we do not identify with them.
Therefore, when they arise,
we watch.
When they pass away,
we remain.

7
Eternal

Hogan

Tao never stops. Why?
Because it isn't trying to accomplish
   anything.

The Masters hang back.
That's why they're ahead of the
   game.

They don't hang on to things.
That's how they manage to keep
   them.

They don't worry about what they
   can't control.
That's why they're always satisfied.

Comments

☯ Mitchell adds an interesting note referring to his use of *detached* in the 2nd stanza. He quotes Bunan: "It is easy to keep things at a distance; it is hard to be naturally beyond them."

☯ Mitchell also comments, referring to his first line calling Tao "*infinite, eternal*: Here is everywhere." This is reminiscent of a Joseph Campbell story about Black Elk. See Further Comments for details and an interesting side note.

☯ The opening line of more traditional translations usually contains references to heaven and earth, with many disparate phrasings. See Further Comments for examples.

8
Sustenance

Mabry

The sagely person is like water
Water benefits all things and does not
  compete with them.
It gathers in unpopular places.
In this it is like the Tao.

> In dwelling, live close to the
>   Earth.

> In thinking, be open to new ideas.

> In relationships, be kind.

> In speech, tell the truth and keep
>   your word.

> In leading people, demonstrate
>   integrity.

> In daily matters, be competent.

> In acting, consider the
>   appropriate timing.

If you do not try to prove yourself
  superior to others,
You will be beyond reproach.

8
Sustenance

Martin 2

Tao is the watercourse way.
It flows through everything,
even the places we find distasteful.
It accepts all things just as they are
and nurtures all without exception.
Were we to live this way
we would live in simple humble
      homes;
we would keep our thoughts upon the
      moment;
we would speak to all with clarity
      and kindness;
we would work at tasks that bring us
      pleasure;
and would take action only when the
      time was right.

8
Sustenance

Beaulac

The highest goodness is like water
which benefits all things, contends
  with none,
and flows into the low places that
  others disdain.
In this, water resembles the Dao.
  In dwelling, what matters is the
    land.
  In thinking, what matters is
    depth.
  In relations with others, what
    matters is taking Heaven's
    view.
  In speaking, what matters is
    sincerity.
  In leadership, what matters is
    harmonious order.
  In work, what matters is
    efficiency.
  In action, what matters is the
    right moment.
Follow the Way that never contends
  and you will be without fault.

Comments

☯ Water is a recurring theme in the Tao Te Ching. Needleman (F&E) notes this and further expands on it: "Water is one of Lao Tsu's principal symbols for the Tao, along with the infant, the female, the valley, and the uncarved block."

☯ Along these lines, similar themes (and further comments) can be seen in verse 78.

☯ There are, unsurprisingly, a number of different variations for the wording of the last line among authors. Perhaps one of the more interesting is Feng & English's: "No fight. No blame" (a much-shortened version of say, Beaulac's [left]).

☯ See Further Comments for thoughts on connections between the first and second halves of the verse.

Beaulac

Grasping a cup and overfilling
is not as good as stopping in time!
If you over-sharpen a blade,
it will dull more quickly.
If you fill a place with gold and jade,
no one can make it safe.
If opulence and rank make you
    important,
you have begun your own downfall.
Be content to complete your task and
    step away from it.
This is the way of Heaven.

Martin

This is a path of letting go
so there will be room to live.

If we hold on to opinions,
our minds will become dull and
    useless.
Let go of opinions.

If we hold on to possessions,
we will always be at risk.
Let go of possessions.

If we hold on to ego,
we will continue to suffer.
Let go of ego.

Working without thought of praise or
    blame
is the way of true contentment.

9
Release

Mair 53

Instead of keeping a bow taut while
  holding it straight,
    better to relax.
You may temper a sword until it is
  razor sharp,
    but you cannot preserve the edge
      for long.
When gold and jade fill your rooms,
  no one will be able to guard them
    for you.
If wealth and honor make you
  haughty,
    you bequeath misfortune upon
      yourself.
To withdraw when your work is
  finished,
    that is the Way of heaven.

Comments

☯ This is one of several warnings about the danger of over-*do*-ing and, indeed, attachment in general. A sort of a Taoist version of "let go and let God," often heard in Christianity. (Remembering, of course, that Taoism and Christianity—or any other religion for that matter—are *not* mutually exclusive!)

☯ As is often the case, several other themes mentioned here are repeated and reinforced in later verses. Mair is one of the few to mention a bow as one of his examples here. This seems to preface the remarks in verse 77 (Balance). For more on stopping in time and the overflowing cup, as in Beaulac's first line, see verses 33 and 46 and the Empty Cup story in the comments of verse 65.

☯ And when it comes to Release, I love Martin's triad of "let go" stanzas in the middle of his version. They speak to me in an elegant way.

Oneness

Mabry

Being both body and spirit,
can you embrace unity and not be
    fragmented?
Being spiritually focused,
can you become soft, like a newborn
    baby?
Being clear in mind and vision,
can you eliminate your flaws?
Loving all people and leading them
    well,
can you do this without imposing
    your will?
When Heaven gives and takes away,
can you be content to just let things
    come or go?
And even when you understand all
    things,
can you simply allow yourself to *be*?

To give birth and nourish,
To make and not own,
To act but not expect something in
    return,
To grow, yet not demand this of
    others,
This is the virtue of Mystery.

10

Oneness

Martin 2

There is only One Life that enlivens
    the Cosmos.
Knowing we are part of this Life
    reveals us as perfect.
Living in this One Life we find our
    true and primal nature.
We become supple, accepting,
    compassionate,
and undisturbed by the way things
    seem to come and go.
Not needing to control, we do not
    become fatigued.
Not needing credit, we work with
    ease and effectiveness.
Our life touches the world with an
    easygoing lightness.
Not clinging to anything, we enjoy
    everything.

10
Oneness

Mitchell

Can you coax your mind from its
    wandering
and keep to the original oneness?
Can you let your body become
supple as a newborn child's?
Can you cleanse your inner vision
until you see nothing but the light?
Can you love people and lead them
without imposing your will?
Can you deal with the most vital
    matters
by letting events take their course?
Can you step back from your own
    mind
and thus understand all things?

Giving birth and nourishing,
having without possessing,
acting with no expectations,
leading and not trying to control:
this is the supreme virtue.

Comments

☯ This verse, to quote Beaulac, "appears to be about abiding in Dao both in meditative stillness and during engagement in activity." In Needleman's (F&E) notes, this is worded as carrying a "hint of the challenge to live fully in the world while maintaining contact with the source . . . embracing the two aspects of reality simultaneously."

☯ Why do I feel like Mitchell's rendition of Lao Tzu's very first question ("Can you coax your mind from its wandering . . .?") is aimed right at me? Ouch. But I am helped in (and coaxed back to) this ongoing practice of quieting the mind by the reminder in these verses that a wandering mind keeps us distracted from experiencing our original Oneness, which is to say our true nature.

☯ Similar thoughts to these show up again in verse 16 (Stillness).

11
Intangible

Mabry

Thirty spokes join together at one
    hub,
But it is the hole in the center that
    makes it operable.

Clay is molded into a pot,
But it is the emptiness inside that
    makes it useful.

Doors and windows are cut to make a
    room,
It is the empty spaces that we use.

Therefore, existence is what we have,
But non-existence is what we use.

11
Intangible

Martin

The spokes and the hub
are the visible parts of a wheel.
The wheel is useful because it spins
    about
the invisible point at its center.

Clay is the material from which a pot
    is made.
The pot is useful because of the
    empty space inside the form.

A house is made with walls, doors,
    and windows.
The house becomes a home for
    people
through the quality of life lived
    within.

We practice with the visible and
    tangible,
but it is the invisible and intangible
    within us
that bring us life.

11
Intangible

Legge

The thirty spokes unite in the one
nave; but it is on the empty
space (for the axle), that the use of
the wheel depends. Clay is
fashioned into vessels; but it is on
their empty hollowness, that
their use depends. The door and
windows are cut out (from the walls)
to form an apartment; but it is on the
empty space (within), that its
use depends. Therefore, what has a
(positive) existence serves for
profitable adaptation, and what has
not that for (actual) usefulness.

Comments

☯ This is the first of my favorite pair
of consecutive verses: They are both
classics of sorts, and they contain
two of my three personal favorite
remarks by Martin.

☯ I'm always struck by what a great
example the clay pot, especially,
makes as something that is not useful
unless it's first *empty*. This leads to
the verse's conclusion, said so
strikingly in Martin: "We practice
with the visible and tangible, but it is
the invisible and the intangible
within us that bring us life." Such a
helpful perspective, at least for me.

☯ At the same time, I sometimes
think we miss the interdependency of
the tangible and Intangible. The
former is indeed made meaningful by
the latter, but the latter has nowhere
to manifest/work without the former.
Interesting. I think Legge's last line
here does a nice job of underlining
this mutual dependency.

12

Internal

Beaulac

The five colors dim one's eyes.
The five musical notes deaden one's
    ears.
The five tastes dull one's palate.
Too much chasing and hunting
    maddens the mind.
Treasured accumulations impede
    one's movement.
Thus, the sage is concerned with the
    inner,
and not with what the eyes see.
He rejects "that out there" and holds
    to "this in here."

12

Internal

Martin

Trying to see everything,
we become blind.
Listening to every voice,
we become confused.
Attempting to satisfy all our appetites
we become weary.
Being driven this way and that
by our conditioning
makes us crazy.
Buying more things
only wastes our energy.

Outer things exist,
but do not define us.
We are mysterious and internal
not obvious and external.

12
Internal

Bynner

The five colors can blind,
The five tones deafen,
The five tastes cloy.
The race, the hunt, can drive men
  mad
And their booty leave them no peace.
Therefore a sensible man
Prefers the inner to the outer eye:
He has his yes,—he has his no.

Comments

☯ Our five senses are among the defining features of our being human. But leaving ourselves open to a constant barrage of sensory input can deaden our perception and clutter our vision.

☯ Looking deeper, the focus in this verse is not so much on sensory desires, it seems, but rather on the inner/outer dichotomy of our true natures.

☯ Martin focuses on this dichotomy in his last stanza, beginning with "Outer things exist, but do not define us." I especially like the last sentence: "We are mysterious and internal not obvious and external."

☯ So an immediate hidden corollary to this is that perhaps senses are not always the best way to *know* the truth(s) of our (inner and outer) worlds.

☯ See Further Comments for more background on the *five colors, tones, and tastes* passages and more.

13
Perspective

Mitchell

Success is as dangerous as failure.
Hope is as hollow as fear.

What does it mean that success is as
   dangerous as failure?
Whether you go up the ladder or
   down it,
your position is shaky.
When you stand with your two feet
   on the ground,
you will always keep your balance.

What does it mean that hope is as
   hollow as fear?
Hope and fear are both phantoms
that arise from thinking of the
   self.
When we don't see the self as self,
what do we have to fear?

See the world as your self.
Have faith in the way things are.
Love the world as your self;
then you can care for all things.

13
Perspective

Martin 2

Don't be concerned with success or
   failure.
Don't worry about your health and
   safety.
The ideas of success and failure keep
   us anxious
and controlled by forces outside
   ourselves.
The idea that we are simply bodies
keeps us isolated and afraid.
Only when we cease striving for
   success,
or struggling to avoid failure,
will we be able to act effectively.
Only when we cease our fear of
   dying,
and know that we are always one
   with all that is,
will we be able to live content.
Only then will we have something to
   give to others.

13
Perspective

Beaulac

"Favor and disgrace: both are
  sources of anxiety."
"Regard great affliction as a
  bodily matter."

What does it mean, "Favor and
  disgrace: both are sources of
  anxiety"?
Favor wanes, so gaining it brings
  anxiety about losing it.
That is why both favor and disgrace
  are sources of anxiety.

What does it mean, "Regard great
  affliction as a bodily matter"?
I can only have great affliction when
  I think I am this body.
When I have realized I am not this
  body, what affliction do I bear?
Try regarding the entire world as
  your body;
then you may be fit to be entrusted
  with the world.
Do so in love, and you are fit to be a
  leader in the world.

Comments

☯ A note in Mair (57.6, 7; 115)
could set the stage for comments
here: "This entire chapter is fraught
with awkward scholarly
explanations."(!) He (Mair) suggests
the original verse may have only
been the first two lines, with the rest
being added commentary. Seems a
stretch to me, but he has a good
point.

☯ And those first two lines are
translated in multiple ways, with
even more variation than usual, it
seems. See Further Comments for
some of them, as well other thoughts.

☯ Martin 2 points out in his
comment that success and failure
"have no meaning outside that we
choose to give them." Hard to
remember!

Mystery

Beaulac

Looking for it, we see nothing and
    call it invisible.
Listening, we hear nothing and call it
    inaudible.
Grasping, there is nothing to get hold
    of and we call it intangible.
Such qualities are beyond scrutiny
    and definitions—
"invisible," "inaudible," and
    "intangible" all dissolve into
    oneness.

This oneness is the One—
in which there is no high and bright
    aspect,
versus some low and dark part
    aspect.
Reaching outward the One is
    limitless;
rebounding, it returns to
    non-existence.
So really this world could be called
    the forms of the Formless,
the shapes of what has no substance.
This is why the *Dao* is called
    "obscure" and "elusive."

Seeking it, we begin nowhere but
    here;
following it, there is nowhere we
    must go.
Holding fast to the timeless Way
you succeed in what is already
    present.
Doing so you penetrate the ancient
    origin, and realize that
this present moment is the continuing
    thread of the Universal Way.

14

Mystery

Martin 2

Reality lies beyond our senses.
We are so used to knowing things
by seeing, hearing, and touching
    them,
that we don't know how to find
the really, truly, Real.
Our mind is fascinating and
    necessary,
but it can't lead us to the Real,
only to ideas about it.
We can only find it
through our inner Self.
Suddenly we see!
Then it slips away
into thoughts about the seeing.
It didn't begin anytime.
It won't go anywhere.
Just breathe and notice your own
    place
in the Eternal Flow.

14
Mystery

Mair 58

We look for it but do not see it;
    we name it "subtle."
We listen for it but do not hear it;
    we name it "rare."
We grope for it but do not grasp it;
    we name it "serene."

These three cannot be fully
    fathomed,
Therefore,
  They are bound together to make
    unity.

Of unity,
    its top is not distant,
    its bottom is not blurred.
Infinitely extended
    and unnameable,
It returns to nonentity.
This is called
    "the form of the formless,
    the image of nonentity."
This is called "the amorphous."

Following behind it,
    you cannot see its back;
Approaching it from the front,
    you cannot see its head.

Hold to the Way of today
    to manage the actualities of
      today,
    thereby understanding the
      primeval beginning.
This is called "the thread of the
  Way."

Comments

☻ This is another verse that points to the innate Mystery of the Tao (without which, it wouldn't be the Tao!).

☻ Though others have similar phrasing, I'm struck by Beaulac's translation of a line in the middle of stanza 2: "So really, this world could be called the forms of the Formless." And his last line in that stanza helps point to the title of Mystery for this verse.

☻ So, as we ponder this unfathomable Mystery, it begins to dawn on me that its very nature speaks to us of its ongoing relevance to our lives in today's world. Since it is beyond even time, it can't go out of date! Or, as Feng & English put it, "Stay with the ancient Tao, / Move with the present."

☻ In the opening three lines, various translations include a phrase similar to Beaulac's or Mair's here: "we call/name it so-and-so." Mair has an interesting note (58.2,4,6) as to the derivation of the terms he uses ("subtle," "rare," and "serene," respectively—see left).

15
Sage

Hogan

The ancient masters were damn
    impressive.
They were deep. Really deep.
Words can't even begin to describe
    how deep they were.
You can only talk about how they
    acted.

They were careful, like a man
    walking on thin ice.
They were cautious, like a soldier
    behind enemy lines.
They were polite, like a guest at a
    party.
They moved quickly, like melting
    ice.
They were as plain as a block of
    wood.
Their minds were as wide as a valley,
and their hearts as clear as spring
    water.

Can you wait for that kind of
    openness and clarity
before you try to understand the
    world?

Can you hold still until events have
    unfolded
before you do the right thing?

When you act without expectations,
you can accomplish great things.

15
Sage

Martin

The freedom of enlightenment
is impossible to describe.
We can only notice how it appears in
    action.

We pay complete attention
to whatever we are doing,
as if we were crossing a river
on ice-covered stones.
We are alert to everything that
    happens,
like a bird watching in all directions.
We have a quiet dignity and reserve,
like a guest who does not seek
    attention.
Our judgments and opinions have
    melted away,
like ice in the summer heat.
There is a beautiful simplicity about
    us,
like a gem before it is shaped and
    polished.
We welcome whatever comes,
as a valley welcomes the river.

To notice this enlightenment,
we sit patiently and wait
for muddy thoughts to settle
and our mind to become clear.
Life then lives itself in us.

Practicing this path, we no longer
    worry
about what we have or don't have
because we have everything!

15
Sage

Bynner

Long ago the land was ruled with a
    wisdom
Too fine, too deep, to be fully
    understood
And, since it was beyond men's full
    understanding,
Only some of it has come down to
    us, as in these sayings:
'Alert as a winter-farer on an icy
    stream,'
'Wary as a man in ambush,'
'Considerate as a welcome guest,'
'Selfless as melting ice,'
'Green as an uncut tree,'
'Open as a valley,'
And this one also, 'Roiled as a
    torrent.'
Why roiled as a torrent?
Because when a man is in turmoil
    how shall he find peace
Save by staying patient till the stream
    clears?
How can a man's life keep its course
If he will not let it flow?
Those who flow as life flows know
They need no other force:
They feel no wear, they feel no tear,
They need no mending, no repair.

Comments

☻ This verse is a rather classic
description of what a *Sage* or *master*
or *the ruling wisdom* looks like in
action. And there are almost as many
variations of these descriptions as
there are translations. (It is
impractical to try to list several, but it
is worth exploring the variety in as
many translations as you might
have.) The ones listed here aren't
quite as traditional, but they give a
feel of both the descriptions and the
variety.

☻ Martin, as is his practice, gives us
his description in the form of what
we would look like, should we
achieve "sagehood." I really like
some of the phrasings here.

☻ Several translations (especially
the more traditional) focus much
more on the "muddy thoughts" theme
briefly mentioned in Martin and the
patience of waiting until mud settles
and the picture clears. Other
translations avoid that angle
completely, or (as Hogan and Bynner
mostly do here) refer to it only
obliquely. In that respect, these three
translations are not quite as
representative.

16
Stillness

Beaulac

Realize emptiness as the utmost
and maintain tranquility as your
  center.
The ten-thousand things arise
  mutually,
and accordingly, return to their one
  Source.
Truly, everything emerges and, after
  growing, returns to its root.
Returning to our Root is tranquil
  stillness;
it is the tranquility of returning to
  one's true nature.
Returning to one's true nature means
  tuning in to the changeless.
Tuning in to the changeless is
  enlightenment.
Not knowing the changeless is the
  delusion which creates misery.

Knowing the changeless makes one
  all-embracing.
    To be all-embracing is to be
      unprejudiced.
    To be unprejudiced is to be truly
      noble.
    To be noble is to be of Heaven.
    To be of Heaven is to be in
      accord with the Dao.
    To be in accord with the Dao
      means to live long, free of peril.

16
Stillness

Mabry

If you can empty yourself of
  everything,
you will have lasting peace.
Things arise, but I contemplate their
  return.
Things flourish and grow, and then
  return to their Source.
To return to the Source is to know
  perfect peace.
I call this a return to Life.

Returning to Life is a Universal
  Constant.
Knowing this is illuminating.
Someone who doesn't understand
  this is in error
and may act dangerously.

But knowing this Constant, you can
  embrace all things.
Embracing all things, you can treat
  them fairly.
Treating them fairly, you are noble.
Being noble, you are like the cosmos.
If you are like the cosmos, you are
  like the Tao.

If you are like the Tao, you will have
  eternal life,
  and you needn't be afraid of dying.

16
Stillness

Martin

When the chatter of our mind quiets
down,
we find the still point
around which all of life revolves.
From this still point we watch
everything
come and go in perfect peace.

Everything that is, was, or ever will
be
has a common source from which it
comes,
in which it lives,
and to which it returns.

Understanding this coming and
going,
we return to our source and our
confusion ends.
Not understanding this, we remain
confused
and bring about great suffering.

Living at the still point, we are open
to all of life.
Open to all of life, we don't judge
anything.
Not judging, we see with
compassion.
Seeing with compassion,
we discover our true nature.
Discovering our true nature,
we are at home
and nothing in life disturbs us.

Comments

☯ Mitchell translates the first line as "Empty your mind of all thoughts," but notes in his comments: "This doesn't mean 'suppress your thoughts,' but 'step back from them.'" He also adds, "Insight into the Tao has nothing to do with the intellect and its abstractions."

☯ On the other hand, Mitchell essentially distinguishes the last comment above from "anti-intellectual" connotations by including one of my favorite remarks from Einstein. See Further Comments.

☯ The various references to emptiness in this verse hit home harder when I recall verse 11 (Intangible). There we are reminded that the clay pot, among other things, is really only useful when it is empty.

☯ I like the flow of the various progressions as they build in the 3rd stanza of Martin and the middle of Beaulac.

17
Leadership

Mitchell

When the Master governs, the
   people
are hardly aware that he exists.
Next best is a leader who is loved.
Next, one who is feared.
The worst is one who is despised.

If you don't trust the people,
you make them untrustworthy.

The Master doesn't talk, he acts.
When his work is done,
the people say, "Amazing:
we did it, all by ourselves!"

17
Leadership

Martin

The deepest virtue is to be unaware
of a separate self at all.
Being aware of a separate self,
it is good to have compassion for that
   self.
Not having compassion for our self,
we become afraid of our own nature.
Being afraid of our own nature,
we come to actually hate our self.
Hating our self,
how can we value anyone else?

Free from self-hate,
our actions are not burdened
by our need for attention.
Therefore people say,
"It happened naturally."

17
Leadership

Mair 61

Preeminent is one whose subjects
   barely know he exists;
The next is one to whom they feel
   close and praise;
The next is one whom they fear;
The lowest is one whom they
   despise.

When the ruler's trust is wanting,
    there will be no trust in him.
Cautious,
   he values his words.
When his work is completed and his
   affairs finished,
    the common people say,
      "We are like this by ourselves."

Comments

☻ An example of a verse where a variety of translations not only exist, but also provide food for thought. Needleman (F&E) calls this a verse about the various qualities of good Leadership, and most traditional authors tend to translate along these lines. Martin, as he often does, makes the focus about the individual self, and Feng & English's actual translation goes ultra-general with no concrete references at all ("The very highest is barely known" and continuing similarly).

☻ Mair also provides his own twist in the last line with his phrasing "We are like this by ourselves," as opposed to "we *did it* by ourselves."

☻ Mitchell provides the interesting thought in his notes that this is "one of several chapters that are as relevant to child-rearing as to government."

☻ In my earliest notes (written all around margins in my first copy of Martin years back), I can tell I thought this was one of the places Martin might have stretched a little by moving a focus to the self, especially in a classic verse about leadership. I think now I have moved to a spot where I treasure (even seek) —and profit from—both viewpoints.

18
Authentic

Mabry

When the great Tao is abandoned,
Ideas of "humanitarianism" and
   "righteousness" appear.
When intellectualism arises
It is accompanied by great hypocrisy.

When there is strife within a family
Ideas of "brotherly love" appear.

When a nation is plunged into chaos
Politicians become "patriotic."

18
Authentic

Martin

When we forget who we truly are,
we turn to external rules
to define goodness and morality.
When we no longer live from our
   heart,
we search for clever strategies
to guide our actions.
This is only a pretense of life.

Duty and loyalty become substitutes
for our inability to love ourselves
and others.
Then we insist our leaders heal the
   suffering
created by our own divided minds.

18
Authentic

Breed

When the Great Way ceased to be
observed,
benevolence and righteousness came
into vogue.
Next came knowledge and
shrewdness,
followed by great hypocrisy.
When harmony no longer prevailed
in the family,
loyal sons and daughters stepped up
to claim their importance.
When the country fell into disorder,
patriotism appeared on the scene.

Comments

☯ Most authors agree that verses 17–20 are similar, but not all agree as to details of the similarity. Red Pine (1996, 37) says 18 is likely a continuation of 17, while Needleman (F&E) groups 18–20 and says they affirm "the primacy of being at one with the Tao." Legge links 17–19, while Mair (63.15–16; 116–117) has specific thoughts about the last two lines, as well as various verse divisions and related facts.

☯ While the words don't immediately indicate this, when I read Martin's version, I continually get an underlying *feeling* that led me to the title: Be real, be genuine, be Authentic.

19
Centered

Mitchell

Throw away holiness and wisdom,
and people will be a hundred times
    happier.
Throw away morality and justice,
and people will do the right thing.
Throw away industry and profit,
and there won't be any thieves.

If these three aren't enough,
just stay at the center of the circle
and let all things take their course.

19
Centered

Martin

If we give up our attempts to be holy
    and wise,
everyone, including ourselves,
will greatly benefit.
If we give up our rules for goodness
    and justice,
all beings will naturally be treated
with loving-kindness.
If we give up striving to accumulate
    by clever means,
theft will disappear.

But these lessons are mere outward
    forms.
The core of our path is this:
we see through our conditioned mind
and find our true nature waiting.

19
Centered

Legge

If we could renounce our sageness
and discard our wisdom, it would be
better for the people a hundredfold. If
we could renounce our benevolence
and discard our righteousness, the
people would again become filial and
kindly. If we could renounce our
artful contrivances and discard our
(scheming for) gain, there would be
no thieves nor robbers.

Those three methods (of government)
Thought olden ways in elegance did
    fail
And made these names their want of
    worth to veil;
But simple views, and courses plain
    and true
Would selfish ends and many lusts
    eschew.

Comments

☻ None of the three translations
chosen here treats the last stanza
quite like most others, where the
focus is on the three external
attributes in the verse, while further
suggesting three (varying forms of)
internal attributes that are, instead,
more worthy of our attention.

☻ Nonetheless, both Mitchell and
Martin provide nice, succinct
summaries of the same thoughts and
may indeed be more helpful.

☻ See the comment in verse 18 for
discussion of the interrelatedness of
verses 17–20.

20
Free

Mabry

Forget ambitious acquisition of
    knowledge,
and your sorrows will end.
How much difference is there between
    "yes" and "no"?
What is the distinction between "good"
    and "evil"?
Must I value what others value?
    Nonsense!
Having no end to their desires, they are
    desolate.

People rush here and there, maybe going
    to a feast,
or perhaps climbing a tower in the
    springtime.
I alone am calm and unconcerned.
Like an unselfconscious infant
At peace and having no destination.

Most people have more than they need.
But I alone seem lost and out of place.
I have the mind of a fool—so confused!

Ordinary people are bright.
I alone seem dim.
Ordinary people are discriminating.
I alone am ambivalent.

        As quiet as the ocean.
        As free as the wind.

People rush about on their very
    important business.
But I alone seem incorrigible and
    uncouth.
I am different from ordinary people;
I enjoy feeding from the Great Mother's
    breasts.

20
Free

Martin

We always strive to make the right
    choice,
and always fear the wrong choice.
We pursue what others say is good,
and avoid what others say is bad.
How sad this is for us!
People are constantly stirred up
like children at a circus—
always looking for the next act to
    entertain them.
But this practice asks us to remain
    undisturbed,
and watch all things
with the detached interest of a
    newborn.

In a culture where excess
    accumulation is the norm,
this path seems idiotic.
Fearful voices in our mind warn us
that we will end up wandering the
    street,
homeless and alone.
We are urged to be clever and
    successful
and always in control.
But this practice asks us to relinquish
    the illusion of control
and to be content with whatever
    comes our way.

This seems so strange
and different from the usual way.
But it is the way of life itself.

20
Free

Hogan

Don't spend too much time thinking
    about stupid shit.
Why should you care if people agree
    or disagree with you?
Why should you care if others find
    you attractive or not?
Why should you care about things
    that worry others?
Call bullshit on all that.

Let other people get worked up and
    try to enjoy themselves.
I'm not going to give myself away.
A baby doesn't know how to smile,
    but it's still happy.

Let other people get excited about
    stuff.
I'm not going to hang on to anything.
I'm not going to fill my mind with
    ideas.
I'm not going to get stuck in a rut,
    tied down to any one place.

Other people are clever;
I guess I must be stupid.
Other people have goals;
I guess I must be aimless.
Like the wind. Or the waves.

I'm not like other people.
I'm getting right with Tao.

Comments

☯ I call this one my "woe is me" classic. It is one of the ones I still struggle with. I've seen viable, even helpful, explanations, but the tone itself is still puzzling to me: Is he bragging or complaining?

☯ I do continue to find Martin's rendition helpful, however.

☯ And Hogan is always interesting. Here, he certainly makes you sit up and take notice right from the get-go.

☯ Some translations lead with some variation of "be done with knowing," while others (if they use it at all) put that at the end of verse 19.

☯ Ellen Chen (1989, 103) calls this verse "a mystic's self-portrayal." I like this, but I guess I still wonder *what* is being portrayed?

Origin

Mabry

The only virtue worth having is that
  of following the Tao,
and the only thing you can say about
  the Tao,
is that it is elusive and evasive.

It is elusive and evasive, yet it can be
  observed.
It is evasive and elusive, yet it does
  manifest itself.
It is dim and dark, yet its essence can
  be grasped.

  Its essence is unquestionably
    genuine.
  You can put your faith in it.

From the beginning of time until the
  present,
its Name has remained.
In it one can see all of Creation.
How do I know where all of Creation
  comes from?
I know the Tao!

21

Origin

Martin 2

How can we let the Tao be our
  guide?
It is without form, elusive, vague.
What is there to hold on to? Is it even
  real?
We can let our desires be without
  form as well,
ephemeral, wispy, not to be grasped.
The Tao's elusiveness
prevents it from becoming an idol.
Its vagueness keeps us mindful of the
  moment
and alert to what is happening now.
The Tao opened the quantum
  mystery
and Big Banged the universe into
  form.
How can we know the Way?
Look deeply. What do you see?

21
Origin

Beaulac

The actions of real virtue and real
    effectiveness
are drawn from the Dao alone.
How is it that the Dao becomes a
    Universe of things?
The Dao's becoming any manifest
    thing is blurred and elusive;
Blurred and elusive, it nevertheless
    contains images of form.
Elusive and indistinct, but from its
    core matter arises.
Secret and obscure!
Yet in it is the vital force.
This vital force is quite genuine;
its evidence is in everything.
That is why, from this moment back
    to ancient times,
its manifesting has never ceased.
So, follow that from which
    everything comes.
How do we recognize that from
    which everything comes?
Through everything as it is right
    now.

Comments

☯ The verse is an interesting mixture of the topics of origins, oneness with all-that-is, living, and the like. Even with the "elusive/blurred/evasive" references, the feeling that comes through for me strongest is "Look at Nature and look within."

☯ The last question ("How do I know where all of Creation comes from?"—Mabry), though phrased differently in almost every translation, is perhaps the oldest in all of mankind: How can I know the Truth?

☯ And the answer, no matter the translation, seems reminiscent of Yahweh's "I Am That I Am" in the Old Testament (Exodus 3:14, KJV).

22
Acceptance

Mitchell

If you want to become whole,
let yourself be partial.
If you want to become straight,
let yourself be crooked.
If you want to become full,
let yourself be empty.
If you want to be reborn,
let yourself die.
If you want to be given everything,
give everything up.

The Master, by residing in the Tao,
sets an example for all beings.
Because he doesn't display himself,
people can see his light.
Because he has nothing to prove,
people can trust his words.
Because he doesn't know who he is,
people recognize themselves in him.
Because he has no goal in mind,
everything he does succeeds.

When the ancient Masters said,
"If you want to be given everything,
give everything up,"
they weren't using empty phrases.
Only in being lived by the Tao
can you be truly yourself.

22
Acceptance

Martin

Accepting what is, we find it to be
    perfect.
What seemed distorted is seen as
    true.
What seemed lacking is seen as
    abundant.
What seemed worn out is seen as
    fresh and new.

Possessing little, we are content.
Too much stuff and we lose our way.

When we reside at the center,
our actions nurture all things.
We don't act out of ego needs,
so our actions are enlightened.
We don't claim to be perfect,
so our ideas are welcomed.
We aren't looking for reward,
so our teaching is enduring
and accessible to all.
We don't try to control or convince
    anyone,
so opposition is not an issue.

"Accept what is,
and find it to be perfect"
is not an idle phrase.
Acceptance of life
is the only path to wholeness.

22
Acceptance

Beaulac

Bend so you remain whole.
Bow, and be lifted upright.
Be empty so you may be filled.
Expend energy and you will be
    renewed.
Have little and you will gain.
But have too much and you just
    become confused.

The sages hold to the One and are
like shepherds for all below Heaven:
    Not standing in their own light
        they shine clearly.
    Not self-righteous they are
        respected.
    Not boasting they have merit.
    Not self-approving they lead.
Competing with no one, no one can
    compete with them.
When the ancients said, "Bend so
    you remain whole"
These were not just idle words.
True wholeness is in returning.

Comments

☯ I have always *really* liked Martin's opening line: "Accepting what is, we find it to be perfect." Now, if I could only assimilate it.

☯ In one of my notes in Martin, I have, "But 'the way it is' is often subjective. And ironically, accepting *that* can change it!" I can't tell if I still believe that, but I like it.

☯ I also like Mitchell's "being lived by the Tao" phrase. In his notes, he compares it to the mother who tells her child to stop sneezing. The boy replies, "I'm *not* sneezing. *It's* sneezing *me!*"

☯ Or for that matter (and Mitchell notes this as well), the phrase is similar to the words of Paul of Tarsus in the New Testament: "Not I, but Christ . . . in me" (Galatians 2:20, KJV).

☯ This verse strikes me as one of those where different translations can give significantly different impressions.

<p style="text-align:center">23
Natural

Mitchell

Express yourself completely,
then keep quiet.
Be like the forces of nature:
when it blows, there is only wind;
when it rains, there is only rain;
when the clouds pass, the sun shines
    through.

If you open yourself to the Tao,
you are at one with the Tao
and you can embody it completely.
If you open yourself to insight,
you are at one with insight
and you can use it completely.
If you open yourself to loss,
you are at one with loss
and you can accept it completely.

Open yourself to the Tao,
then trust your natural responses;
and everything will fall into place.

23
Natural

Martin 2

Why so much concern over what to
    do,
and what to say, and how to act?
Stay still, without a need to interfere.
When it rains, it rains.
When it stops raining, it stops.
You are a force of nature
no less than the clouds and oceans.
When it is time to speak,
you will naturally speak.
When it is time to act,
you will naturally act.
Mostly you will be still and quiet.
Then life will be a seamless whole,
flowing from moment to moment
    without effort.

23
Natural

Hogan

When you have nothing to say,
you may as well keep your mouth
   shut.
The wind and the rain don't go on
   forever.
If nature knows enough to give it a
   rest sometimes,
so should you.

If you're ready for Tao, you can live
   with Tao.
If you're ready to succeed, you can
   live with success.
If you're ready to fail, you can live
   with failure.

Trust your instincts,
and others will trust you.

Comments

☯ As part of a long and excellent note, Needleman (F&E) calls this verse "perhaps the most puzzling in the whole of the *Tao Te Ching*," and follows that with a humorous quote by Richard Wilheim. See Further Comments for more.

☯ For me, Martin 2 comes closest to capturing the gist of the message, while also underlining and connecting it to the Taoist oneness with nature (which is not *quite* the same as Natural). On the other hand, the oneness expressed here ("When it is time to speak [act], you will naturally speak [act]"), while wholly desirable, still seems like a distant goal for me.

☯ In his accompanying note, Martin 2 also points out similarities between this verse and the sermon on the mount in the Bible, and adds, "I always thought Jesus was a Taoist anyway."

☯ I like the feel of Mitchell's "If you open yourself to . . ." trilogy in the second stanza. It feels more inviting to me, and even the comment about loss doesn't feel as negative as other translations, for some reason.

24
Excess

Beaulac

Lifted on tiptoes, one cannot
  stand firm.
With too big a stride, one cannot
  walk far.
One who flaunts himself does not
  really shine.
One who is self-approving is not
  really superior.
Boasting about oneself reveals no
  actual merit.
One who is self-important does
  not endure.

From the perspective of the Way,
these are like rotting leftovers to be
  thrown out, or useless activity.
In nature, creatures avoid such waste.
A person of the Way does not live
  like that.

24
Excess

Martin

Stretching to reach it,
we fall.
Running to catch it,
we get lost.
Pretending to be enlightened,
we become dim and foolish.
Trying to "do it right,"
we fail.
Looking for praise,
we receive nothing.
Grabbing hold of it,
we lose it.

All of this strutting, striving,
straining, and grasping
is excess baggage.
The very freedom it promises does
  not appear
until we lay it down.

24
Excess

Feng & English

He who stands on tiptoe is not
    steady.
He who strides cannot maintain the
    pace.
He who makes a show is not
    enlightened.
He who is self-righteous is not
    respected.
He who boasts achieves nothing.
He who brags will not endure.
According to followers of the Tao,
    "These are extra food and
    unnecessary luggage."
They do not bring happiness.
Therefore followers of the Tao avoid
    them.

Comments

☯ Beaulac and Martin—different as
they are—seem to synergistically
complement each other in stressing
the theme of Excess.

☯ In this verse, I also hear
corresponding themes: *Don't over-
DO.* Don't get out of balance. *Be. Let
the Tao.*

☯ Feng & English's "extra food and
unnecessary luggage" line presents
an effective image. I also appreciate
their last two lines, which somehow
seem less harsh, perhaps, than other
translations.

25
Tao

Mitchell

There was something formless and
   perfect
before the universe was born.
It is serene. Empty.
Solitary. Unchanging.
Infinite. Eternally present.
It is the mother of the universe.
For lack of a better name,
I call it the Tao.

It flows through all things,
inside and outside, and returns
to the origin of all things.

The Tao is great.
The universe is great.
Earth is great.
Man is great.
These are the four great powers.

Man follows the earth.
Earth follows the universe.
The universe follows the Tao.
The Tao follows only itself.

Martin 2

Since before the beginning of
   beginning-less time,
Something stood formless, tranquil,
   and solitary.
The Source of all form,
it itself is formless.
Like the womb from which the
   Cosmos had its birth.
It has no name.
Giving it a name is foolish
but, foolish me, I call it Tao.
It can be seen in the Cosmos,
from which our Earth was formed.
It can be seen in the Earth
from which we were formed.
And it makes its home within all
   things,
including each of us.

25
Tao

Breed

There was something undefined and
complete,
coming into existence before Heaven
and Earth.
How still it was and formless,
standing alone, and undergoing no
change,
reaching everywhere and in no
danger of ever being exhausted!
Think of it as the Mother of all
things.
I do not know its name, so I call it
the Tao, the Way.
If I try even harder to use words to
describe it,
I call it only the Wonderful.
Wonderful, it passes on in constant
flow.
Passing on, it becomes distant.
Having become distant, it returns.
Therefore the Tao is wonderful;
Heaven is wonderful; Earth is
wonderful;
and the wise person is also
wonderful.
In the universe there are four things
that are wonderful,
and the wise person is one of them.
People take their law from the Earth;
the Earth takes its law from Heaven;
Heaven takes its law from the Tao.
The law of the Tao is simply what it
is.

Comments

☻ This is one of the verses that
reinforces the vast, nameless,
indescribable sense of *awe* that the
Tao embodies. It is often lying
underneath other themes, but the
more I read the Tao Te Ching, the
more it seems to be bubbling to the
surface. (See similar comments in
verse 72 [Awe].) This sense of awe
also seems to go hand-in-hand with
the inability to accurately *describe*
the Tao.

☻ Similarly, I was highly intrigued
by part of a comment in Martin 2's
notes: After noting Lao Tzu's
attempts to describe the majesty of
the Tao, he also notes Lao Tzu's
reluctance to name it (the Tao), as
"he realizes that it may be
misunderstood and morphed into a
God-like concept." Most interesting.
As one of my spiritual mentor friends
used to say, "To get to God, you have
to give up [your limiting ideas of]
God."

☻ At the end of the verse, most
translations list the four great things.
The first three are commonly called
the Tao, Heaven, and Earth. The
fourth, however, is not uniformly
named. Some label it "Man" in
general; some use a more specific
"wise person" or "person of the
Tao"; and many of the more
traditional translations still use
"ruler" or "king."

26
Grounded

Breed

Lightness can't exist without gravity.
Quietness is the master of
restlessness.
Therefore the wise person travels an
entire day
without leaving beyond her supplies.
Even though she looks at luxurious
sights,
she remains composed, indifferent.
How can someone who has many
vehicles
take the world lightly?
Don't lose your grounding.
If you are restless, you lose your
authority.

26
Grounded

Martin 2

A deeply rooted path allows a
light-hearted life.
A stable path quiets restlessness.
No matter where we go,
we are still at home.
Even though distractions abound,
our mind does not flit about,
always looking for something else.
There is nothing we need
that we do not already have.
Urgent demands clamor
for the attention of our mind,
yet we remain calm and centered.

26
Grounded

Beaulac

The weighty is root of the light;
and the serene is ruler of the
  restless.
Just so, a noble person may travel
  all day
and not leave behind his supplies.
In his protected camp he is at ease
  and unconcerned.
Would a king over ten thousand
  chariots take *himself* more lightly
than he does the empire?
    Frivolous actions stray from the
      Source;
    Restlessness strays from
      self-mastery.

Comments

☯ All three of the chosen selections here seem to eloquently (if not at all similarly!) reinforce the need for the Taoist seeker to be Grounded. It seems that this is a call to be rooted *in the Tao* and should *not* be confused with a connotation of being overly serious about daily happenings or surroundings. Indeed, reinforcing that, I like Martin 2's opening line, "A deeply rooted path allows a light-hearted life."

☯ In that vein, I believe it to be a mistake to confuse this verse (or the Tao Te Ching in general) to be an admonition against travel, as is often done. Perhaps this is a pet-peeve-like fixation of mine, as it will surface a couple more times (see verses 47 and 80, for cxample.)

27
Open

Mitchell

A good traveler has no fixed plans
and is not intent upon arriving.
A good artist lets his intuition
lead him wherever it wants.
A good scientist has freed himself of
    concepts
and keeps his mind open to what is.

Thus the Master is available to all
    people
and doesn't reject anyone.
He is ready to use all situations
and doesn't waste anything.
This is called embodying the light.

What is a good man but a bad man's
    teacher?
What is a bad man but a good man's
    job?
If you don't understand this, you will
    get lost,
however intelligent you are.
It is the great secret.

27
Open

Martin

This path has no rules, no rituals,
and no preconceived notions.
Traveling it we seek neither praise
    nor blame,
yet our actions become impeccable
    and blameless.

Our life is illumined by the light.
Everything that happens
is for our benefit.
Everything in our experience
instructs us in the way.
Everyone we meet becomes our
    teacher,
good and bad alike.
Everyone we meet becomes our
    student,
bright and dull alike.
If we try to pick and choose,
we will never learn.

Ceasing to pick and choose:
this is the great secret of life.

27
Open

Beaulac

The true journey leaves neither
tracks nor trace.
True speech is beyond fault or
fault-finding.
True reckoning requires neither
math nor record-keeping.
True shutting needs neither bolt
nor bar, yet cannot be opened.
True binding requires neither
rope nor twine, yet cannot be undone.

This is the level of skill a sage uses
in saving people;
He rejects no one, nothing useful is
abandoned.
This is called following one's light.
In such practice, the good person is
simply a teacher,
and the bad person is the good
person's raw material.
But without honoring the teacher as
such
or caring for the raw material as
such,
any learning is great confusion.
This is seeing through to the essence.

Comments

☯ In his notes, Mitchell calls this
"one of the most important chapters
in the Tao Te Ching."

☯ I've often been puzzled by the
good person/bad person/teacher
references in the 2nd stanza. (See
more thoughts in Further Comments,
as well as verse 62.) I really like the
way Martin (see facing page) avoids
these labels entirely, but in the
process, this misses the more usual
discussion in the 2nd stanza of how
the sage/master saves or takes care of
(or is there for) all people.

☯ Beaulac also does a nice job of
phasing here, and I particularly like
his "This is the level of skill . . ."
sentence as an effective link between
the thoughts of the 1st and 2nd
stanzas. And, his "honoring" wording
near the end seems to take some of
the sting out of the good/bad labels.

☯ Martin's first two "Everything"
lines in the 2nd stanza really speak to
me. Do I/we dare to believe them?
Regardless of your own answer to
that, it makes an interesting thought
experiment to consider how our lives
would be affected if we could
manifest the lines' truth into our
daily lives!

☯ See the Further Comments for
different renditions of the last lines of
the 2nd and 3rd stanzas.

28
Receptive

Mabry

Know the active, the masculine
Yet keep to the passive, the feminine
And you will cradle the World.
If you lovingly hold the World
You will know eternal goodness
And will become again as a little
  child.

Be aware of the obvious—the light
But keep to the mysterious—the dark
And set an example for the world.
Be an example for the world
And do not stray from your calling
And you will return to the Eternal.

Know honor, yet remain humble
And be empty of the world.
Being empty of the world is good
  enough
And you will return to the simplicity
  of the uncarved block.
If the block is carved it is trapped in
  one form and critiqued.
The Sage prefers simplicity and so is
  ahead of them all.
He knows better than to divide the
  whole.

28
Receptive

Martin 2

Repression of the primal energy
  within us
leaves us divided against ourselves.
When our successes are joined with
  our failures;
When our words rest upon our
  silence;
When our actions arise from our
  stillness;
when our heart is wedded with our
  mind;
then the power of the Tao will flow
  unhindered through us.
Without the unity of opposing forces,
  life becomes a constant battle.
Many leaders thrive upon this
  division,
turning one against the other
to consolidate power and profit.
But the one who holds the Unity
  complete
will not be fooled by clever words,
and can see the virtue in all things.

28
Receptive

Mitchell

Know the male,
yet keep to the female:
receive the world in your arms.
If you receive the world,
the Tao will never leave you
and you will be like a little child.

Know the white,
yet keep to the black:
be a pattern for the world.
If you are a pattern for the world,
the Tao will be strong inside you
and there will be nothing you can't
    do.

Know the personal,
yet keep to the impersonal:
accept the world as it is.
If you accept the world,
the Tao will be luminous inside you
and you will return to your primal
    self.

The world is formed from the void,
like utensils from a block of wood.
The Master knows the utensils,
yet keeps to the the block:
thus she can use all things.

Comments

☯ Mitchell's three stanzas succeed for me and seem to provide a flow to the entire verse that some others don't quite capture. Yet, I also appreciate the way Martin 2's rendition effectively brings some clarity to and effective blending of the sets of dualities here. And I believe that this "blending" is a large part of the theme of this verse.

☯ In Mitchell's note he also further relates the *Receptive* in stanza 1 to the *creative*: "Keeping to the receptive allows the creative to arise. Actually the creative and the receptive are complementary sides of the same process." Nice observation. (See the last comment in verse 6 for a similar remark by Mitchell.)

☯ We have encountered other mentions and images of the interrelatedness of the feminine, creative, Receptive, uncarved blocks and more. See comments for verses 6 and 8, for example.

29
Flow

Mitchell

Do you want to improve the world?
I don't think it can be done.

The world is sacred.
It can't be improved.
If you tamper with it, you'll ruin it.
If you treat it like an object, you'll
    lose it.

There is a time for being ahead,
a time for being behind;
a time for being in motion,
a time for being at rest;
a time for being vigorous,
a time for being exhausted;
a time for being safe,
a time for being in danger.

The Master sees things as they are,
without trying to control them.
She lets them go their own way,
and resides at the center of the circle.

29
Flow

Martin

Attempting to control external events
will never keep us safe.
Control is an illusion.

Whatever we try to control,
we separate from ourselves.
Whatever we try to fix,
we ruin.
Life is sacred,
and flows exactly as it should.

We return to our breathing.
It knows exactly what to do,
rising and falling without conscious
    control.
In the same way
we sometimes have an excess
and sometimes have a lack.
We sometimes assert ourselves,
and sometimes hold back.
We sometimes succeed,
and sometimes fail completely.

Our practice is to see all this
without taking it seriously.
That way we do not abandon
    ourselves.
We remain at peace.

29
Flow

Feng & English

Do you think you can take over the
    universe and improve it?
I do not believe it can be done.

The universe is sacred.
You cannot improve it.
If you try to change it, you will ruin
    it.
If you try to hold it, you will lose it.

So sometimes things are ahead and
    sometimes they are behind;
Sometimes breathing is hard,
    sometimes it comes easily;
Sometimes there is strength and
    sometimes weakness;
Sometimes one is up and sometimes
    down.

Therefore the sage avoids extremes,
    excesses, and complacency.

Comments

☻ This verse, especially as expressed in the last stanza of both Martin and Mitchell, strikes me as a succinct definition of wisdom for the Taoist.

☻ I have chosen the title Flow for this verse, as that seems to be the major theme. ("Life is sacred, and flows exactly as it should."—Martin) But I can't help also feeling a sense of *moderation* here, not only as it refers to our own internal still point in the midst of life, but also as a reference to moderation akin to the Buddhist sense of "the Middle Way."

☻ It seems impossible to read the second stanza (regardless of translator) without thinking of the similar "For everything there is a season" passage in Ecclesiastes 3:1–8 (NSRV).

☻ The more I read this verse in its various versions (especially Martin's), the more I *also* feel the verse is as much (or more) about dropping our need to control things in our environment (and—hence—letting it Flow), as it is about bettering the world. See verse 30 for similar thoughts.

30
Overdoing

Mitchell

Whoever relies on the Tao in
    governing men
doesn't try to force issues
or defeat enemies by force of arms.
For every force there is a
    counterforce.
Violence, even well intentioned,
always rebounds upon oneself.

The Master does his job
and then stops.
He understands that the universe
is forever out of control,
and that trying to dominate events
goes against the current of the Tao.
Because he believes in himself,
he doesn't try to convince others.
Because he is content with himself,
he doesn't need others' approval.
Because he accepts himself,
the whole world accepts him.

30
Overdoing

Martin 2

Every force is met
with an opposing force.
Leaders who follow the Tao never
    force their will,
and never seek to defeat their
    opponents.
Battles do not bring victory,
only misery for all involved.
A follower of the Tao does what
    needs doing without undue effort.
He isn't worried about reward.
He knows when to stop, and stops
    completely.
We can do things with great struggle
and they will sometimes seem
    impressive,
but they will not last.
The struggle holds them together,
when the struggle stops
they disintegrate.
Only natural work endures.

30
Overdoing

Hogan

Listen up: If you want to be a leader
who's in touch with Tao,
never use violence to achieve your
goals.

Every act of violence backfires.
An army on the move leaves a trail of
tears,
and a military victory always lies in
ruins.

The Masters do what needs doing
and that's all they do.
Do what you have to do without
arrogance or pride.
Get the job done and don't brag
about it afterwards.
Do what you have to do,
not for your own benefit,
but because it needs to be done.
And don't do it the way you think it
should be done,
do it the way it needs to be done.

The mighty will always lose their
power
and any connection they ever had to
Tao.
They will not last long;
if you're not right with Tao, you
might as well be dead.

Comments

☯ Like so many verses in the Tao Te
Ching (see verses 31 and 69, for
example), this one begins as another
lesson in good governance, with
warnings about unwise use of force,
specifically military. But as
evidenced by all three translations
here, it quickly expands and is easily
adaptable to not only leadership in
general, but to the effective living of
a good life.

☯ And there are the frequent touches
of *wu-wei* in all contexts, with a
warning against *Over*-doing: "The
Masters do what needs doing and
that's all they do" (Hogan).

☯ In the context of knowing when to
stop, Mitchell's translation notes that
"The Master . . . understands that the
universe is forever out of control."
These days *out of control* frequently
carries a connotation of chaotic, but I
think it would be a mistake to apply
that here. Instead, it appears to echo
verse 29, where learning to relinquish
our need to control actually helps the
Tao do its work (especially in
Nature?!). See similar comments on
knowing when to stop in verse 32.

31
Peace

Mabry

All weapons are bad news
And all creatures should detest them.
So those who follow the Tao do not keep
them.

(Wise people prefer the left side as the
place of honor,
but the General always stands on the
right.)

Weapons are the tools of fear.
They are not appropriate for a
Sage
And should only be one's last
resort.
Peace is always far superior.

There is no beauty in victory.
To find beauty in it would be to rejoice
at killing people.
Anyone who delights in slaughter will
never find
satisfaction in this world.

(When celebrating happy occasions,
the left side is the place of honor,
But on unhappy occasions, the right is
preferred.
Then we see those of lower rank
standing on the left;
The General is given the right-hand
position.)

Military officers should observe their
duties gravely,
For when many people are killed
They should be mourned with great
sorrow.
Celebrate your victory only with funeral
rites.

31
Peace

Breed

Weapons, however beautifully
crafted,
are instruments of evil.
All creatures hate them.
Therefore, those who follow the Tao
do not use weapons.
Ordinarily, the wise person considers
the left hand—the feminine quality—
the most honorable place,
but in time of war, people value more
the right hand—the masculine
quality.
Sharp weapons are instruments of
evil, however,
and a wise person turns to them
only when they are absolutely
necessary.
Instead, the wise person values calm
and peace.
Victory through force is meaningless.
To think otherwise would mean
to delight in human slaughter.
The person who delights in slaughter
brings discord to the world.
In times of celebration, the masculine
quality is prized.
During times of mourning, the
feminine quality is valued.
The second-in-command of the army
has his place on the left,
while the general has his on the right,
a place of mourning.
The person who has killed in battle
should weep
with bitterest grief for those who
have lost their lives.
A victory in battle is like a funeral.

31
Peace

Feng & English

Good weapons are instruments of
    fear; all creatures hate them.
Therefore followers of Tao never use
    them.
The wise man prefers the left.
The man of war prefers the right.

Weapons are instruments of fear;
    they are not a wise man's tools.
He uses them only when he has no
    choice.
Peace and quiet are dear to his heart,
And victory no cause for rejoicing.
If you rejoice in victory, then you
    delight in killing;
If you delight in killing, you cannot
    fulfill yourself.

On happy occasions precedence is
    given to the left,
On sad occasions to the right.
In the army the general stands on the
    left,
The commander-in-chief on the right.
This means that war is conducted like
    a funeral.
When many people are being killed,
They should be mourned in heartfelt
    sorrow.
That is why a victory must be
    observed like a funeral.

Comments

☯ Continuing from verse 30, this verse is a strong, uncompromising indictment of weapons, in particular, and some even include the military in general.

☯ Even though the Tao Te Ching does not condone the waging of war (see verse 69), there seems to be latitude for a military for defense purposes.

☯ This is somewhat condensed, but during the times of the Tao Te Ching, the right hand (which usually holds the sword) was considered more aggressive/masculine while the left hand (holding the warrior's shield) represented non-aggressive/passivity or the more feminine side.

☯ I can't help sensing an undercurrent of a broader oft-repeated theme here. Pulled from the context of this verse, Breed's wording, "the wise person values calm and peace. Victory through force is meaningless," would seem to fit nicely in other verses as well. See verse 79, for example, where these sentiments are applied more directly to relationships.

32

Distinctions

Mabry

The Tao will always be beyond
   comprehension.
Although it seems trivial
No one in all the world can control it.

If governments and leaders can abide
   in it
All beings shall gratefully behave
   likewise.
We would have a Heaven on Earth
And sweet rains would fall.
The people would not need to be
   told,
They would just naturally do what is
   right.

When you organize, you must of
   necessity
use names and order.
But given that, you must also know
   where to leave off
naming and structuring.
Knowing when to stop, you can
   avoid danger.
All the World is to the Tao
As rivers flowing home to the sea.

32

Distinctions

Martin

What we call the Tao
really has no name.
Naming something, we think we
   understand it.
What we call the Tao is far too subtle
   for that.
We experience it in our own true
   nature.
If we hold on to our own true nature,
all external and internal strife falls
   away.
Peace descends on our lives
like a gentle rain from heaven.
Joy flows from the earth
like a mighty river.
There is no need to urge ourselves
to do good.
Goodness is our heart's true nature.

The more we use words,
the more distinctions we make.
The more distinctions we make,
the more we suffer.
When we stop taking distinctions
   seriously,
we cease to suffer.
We return to peace
just as streams and rivers
return to the ocean.

32
Distinctions

Beaulac

The Way is forever nameless.
Though it is both elementary and
  infinitesimal,
no one in the world has power over
  it.
If princes and kings could hold to it,
all things would yield of their own
  accord.
The harmonizing of Heaven and
  earth
causes a sweet dew to fall on all
  people alike;
peace and harmony ensue not by any
  decree, but spontaneously.
As soon as there are regulations
  things need to be named.
Now that they are named, it's time to
  stop dividing.
Knowing when to stop, you avoid
  danger.

If you want to understand the Dao in
  this world, picture this:
    many rivulets flowing into
      streams,
    streams flowing into great rivers,
    and great rivers flowing into the
      one ocean.

Comments

☻ Interesting thoughts here, not just about naming, but indeed *over-*naming. The authors here (especially Mabry and Beaulac) seem to imply, in their translations, that naming is OK—even needed— *up to a point,* and then we need to learn to STOP naming, that is, making Distinctions. That *stopping point,* unfortunately, seems ill-defined.

☻ Following that up, I think I'm influenced by some notes I found from reading this verse on an earlier time through. The gist: Our ever-increasing Distinctions (dare we say judgments?) trip us up as much as the naming.

☻ Take that a step further and look at the proverbial biblical warning to "Judge not, that ye be not judged" (Matthew 7:1, KJV). If we make Distinctions, which is to say *judgments,* with and among others, then we begin to be increasingly lost in the duality instead of remembering our universal oneness. So, . . . minimize Distinctions (judge not) *lest* we forget our oneness (are judged). Probably not satisfying to a biblical (or Taoist!) scholar, but I think I still like it.

Beaulac

Understanding others is knowledge,
but understanding oneself is
   enlightenment.
Conquering others is merely force;
conquering oneself is true strength.

Knowing what is enough is wealth.
Making right effort shows inner
   resolve.
Holding to one's center, one endures.
Dying with these intact, one is
   immortal.

33
Wisdom

Martin 2

The intelligent person knows about
   things and people.
The wise person knows about
   himself.
The strong person conquers others.
The most powerful person
conquers his own conditioned mind.
The grasping person gathers
   treasures.
The tranquil person already has
   everything.
In the world, long life is valued.
In the Tao, life and death are the
   same.

33
Wisdom

Hogan

Knowing things makes you smart,
but knowing yourself makes you
    wise.
To rule others, you must be powerful,
but to rule yourself, you must be
    strong.

If you have only what you need, you
    have true wealth.
If you never give up, you will find a
    way.
If you stay true to yourself, you will
    never be lost.
If you stay alive your whole life,
    you've really lived.

Comments

☯ For my part, I much prefer translations that talk about *understanding* one's self, as Beaulac does in lines 1 and 2 (but not 3 and 4?), as opposed to *conquering* or *mastering* one's self or one's mind.

☯ Perhaps I'm being picky, but I'm not sure one *conquers* or *masters* one's self—or if that is even the goal! (And, if one masters the self, who is doing the mastering, and who is being mastered?) In this case, understanding one's self seems much more beneficial (and Taoist!) than conquering.

☯ Along those lines, I also like Martin 2's approach of *overcoming our conditioning.* Makes sense to me, and goes hand in hand with understanding.

34
Omnipresent

Mabry

The great Tao flows everywhere,
to the left and to the right.
All things rely on it for their life
and it does not refuse them.
When its work is done, it does not
    demand recognition.
It clothes and nourishes all things
and does not demand allegiance.

Since it makes no demands for itself,
it can seem to be of small regard.
Yet as all things return to it of their
    own accord,
without being commanded, it can
    truly be regarded Great.
It is only because it does not claim to
    be Great
That it is able to achieve such
    Greatness.

34
Omnipresent

Martin 2

The Tao fills the universe with Itself.
All that is, is part of It
and It cannot lose
a single atom of Itself.
Since nothing is outside of It,
It needs no thanks or honor.
It makes no claim of ownership.
It wants nothing from us.
It needs no worship.
No wonder we love it so.
It is our very Self.

34
Omnipresent

Mitchell

The great Tao flows everywhere.
All things are born from it,
yet it doesn't create them.
It pours itself into its work,
yet it makes no claim.
It nourishes infinite worlds,
yet it doesn't hold on to them.
Since it is merged with all things
and hidden in their hearts,
it can be called humble.
Since all things vanish into it
and it alone endures,
it can be called great.
It isn't aware of its greatness;
thus it is truly great.

Comments

☯ Interesting verse! Martin 2's opening sentence in his note on this verse calls it one of the places where the Tao Te Ching "expresses the distinction between the Tao and the common concepts of God," especially in reference to our ideas of God as *out there* or separate from us. Most interesting. It is harder to get an *out there* feeling about the Tao while reading this, isn't it? (See similar thoughts about our *ideas of God* in the comments in verse 25.)

☯ At the same time, as I read verses like this that speak of *it* doing this and that, *it* being considered humble, and so on, I get the feeling of the Tao being given anthropomorphic qualities.

☯ Which in turn leads me to a question I discovered in my notes, related to this verse: "Is the Tao conscious? How *could* it be? How could it *not* be?!" What do *you* think? Discuss among yourselves.

☯ Mitchell has an interesting possible answer/counterpoint to the above question. See Further Comments.

Inexhaustible

Mabry

Whoever holds firmly to following
   the Tao
Will draw all the World to herself.
She may go anywhere and not be
   afraid,
Finding only safety, balance, and
   peace.

Music and good food lure passers-by
But words about the Tao
Seem bland and flavorless to them.

Look, and it cannot be seen.
Listen, and it cannot be heard.
Use it, and it cannot be exhausted.

Inexhaustible

Martin 2

Within the Tao
all forms come and go.
Holding to the forms,
we suffer great loss.
Holding to the Tao,
we are content and happy.
The forms that come and go are
   exciting and compelling,
so we try to grasp them, keep them,
   make them endure
and make them work on our behalf.
We end up exhausted.
The Tao is impossible to grasp,
yet only it can satisfy.

35
Inexhaustible

Beaulac

Hold to the Great Image
and the world will come to you—
come, and not be harmed—
and will enjoy harmony and
    health.

For music and pastries even passing
    folk will stop,
but words about the Way seem plain
    and flavorless.
This is because looked for, it can't
    even be seen,
and listened for, it can't even be
    heard,
but utilized, it is inexhaustible!

Comments

☯ I love some of the images and feelings in this verse, but as may be apparent from these comments (or lack thereof), I still have a hard time identifying, for myself, an underlying theme amidst the various ideas. Perhaps this is one of those places where I shouldn't try as hard. Don't over-search—just listen with the heart?

☯ This would be a good place (along with the other 80 verses!) to decide what the verse is saying to *you*. If you get The Answer on this one, let me know.

☯ I think Martin 2 might come the closest here to unifying these thoughts—at least for me. And Beaulac's ideas are helpful as well.

Perception

Mabry

What you want shrunk
Must first be allowed to expand.

What you want weakened
Must first be strengthened.

What you want destroyed
Must first be allowed to flourish.

That which you want to take
Must first be given.

Seeing this is an understanding of the
  subtle.

What is soft and weak overcomes
  what is hard and strong.

Just as a fish should keep to deep
  waters,
So a country's weapons should be
  kept out of sight,
so as not to tempt people.

36

Perception

Martin 2

If we try to push away our thoughts,
  they will resist us,
and naturally remain.
If we cling to them,
they will be reinforced,
and naturally remain.
If we let them rest
in an open spacious mind, neither
  resisting nor attending,
they will fade into the mists.

36
Perception

Bynner

He who feels punctured
Must once have been a bubble,
He who feels unarmed
Must have carried arms,
He who feels belittled
Must have been consequential,
He who feels deprived
Must have had privilege,
Whereas a man with insight
Knows that to keep under is to
    endure.
What happens to a fish pulled out of
    a pond?
Or to an implement of state pulled
    out of a scabbard?
Unseen, they survive.

Comments

☻ Another occurrence of a collection of apparently contradictory phrases that occur throughout the Tao Te Ching.

☻ I've always been a little puzzled by Lao Tzu's (and/or so many translators') use of the word *must* in the opening lines. It tends to grate on my ears, not only in terms of perceived Taoist tendencies, but also occasionally in terms of formal logic (fallacy of the inverse or converse). Maybe I'm just stubborn?

☻ Red Pine (1996, 72) uses *should* for the *musts*, and Martin 2 (facing page) nicely re-words the whole verse in a softer (and to my mind, more enlightening and less confusing) way.

☻ On the other hand, Bynner's (left) use of "must" as a logical conclusion (rather than imperative), seems to make for an excellent and equally enlightening perspective.

☻ Lao Tzu's apparent out-of-the-blue reference to weapons (see Mabry, for example, and others) seems a little puzzling. I am helped by Bynner's phrasing.

☻ Mabry's "understanding the subtle" is translated in a variety of ways. See Further Comments for some of them.

37
Simplicity

Breed

The Tao in its regular course
does nothing for the sake of doing it,
and so there is nothing it does not do.
If the world's leaders could follow
the Tao,
all things would be transformed.
If this transformation becomes
something I desire,
I will transform even the desire with
a nameless simplicity.
A simplicity without a name is free
from all external aim.
With no desire, it is at rest and still.
Things will naturally take their
proper course.

37
Simplicity

Martin 2

If leaders and officials
could work as the Tao works,
people would be tranquil and content.
Everything needed
would naturally be done.
But leaders and officials
feel the need to push for progress,
patriotism, and greed.
They create dissatisfaction
and keep people stirred up
and angry at each other.
No one understands the way of
effortless living;
of silence and peace;
of true contentment.

37
Simplicity

Mabry

The Tao never "acts"
Yet nothing is left undone.

If the governments and leaders would
    keep it
All things would of their own accord
    be transformed.

Should desires arise from
    transformation
I shall influence them through silent
    simplicity.
Silent simplicity involves being free
    from desires.

When you are without desire you are
    content
And all the World is at peace.

Comments

☯ Somehow, the Taoist ideal of *wu-wei* and our current world governments don't seem to fit in the same sentence, do they? But this verse contains such a nice blueprint! (And Martin 2 seems *so* pertinent in these troublesome times, as well.)

☯ The main theme here seems to be the ever-elusive contentment and "silent simplicity" (Mabry). Breed even titles *his* selection "nameless simplicity."

☯ But as Martin 2 points out, "No one understands the way of effortless living." (Similar thoughts can be seen in verse 70.) And, in his notes, Martin 2 makes an intriguing comment: "Trying to be content is an oxymoron." Interesting paradox—the desire to be content shows that we're not!

☯ I sympathize with Martin 2's renditions of Lao Tzu's lament. I continue to wonder how something so desirable on the surface can be so difficult to allow in practice. Why do we (or at least I!) make it so hard?

38
Virtue

Mitchell

The Master doesn't try to be powerful;
thus he is truly powerful.
The ordinary man keeps reaching for
    power;
thus he never has enough.

The Master does nothing,
yet he leaves nothing undone.
The ordinary man is always doing
    things,
yet many more are left to be done.

The kind man does something,
yet something remains undone.
The just man does something,
and leaves many things to be done.
The moral man does something,
and when no one responds
he rolls up his sleeves and uses force.

When the Tao is lost, there is goodness.
When goodness is lost, there is
    morality.
When morality is lost, there is ritual.
Ritual is the husk of true faith,
the beginning of chaos.

Therefore the Master concerns himself
with the depths and not the surface,
with the fruit and not the flower.
He has no will of his own.
He dwells in reality,
and lets all illusions go.

38
Virtue

Martin 2

Trying to be good is not virtuous.
To help without knowing it is doing
    good,
that is true virtue.
Without the Tao, we try to learn to be
    virtuous.
When we fail at being virtuous,
we learn the rules of kindness.
When we fail at kindness,
we are subject to the rules of fairness.
When we fail at fairness,
we are subject to the rules of justice.
All these rules are confusing
and lead only to empty rituals and
    misery.
The master lives without rules
and follows only his own true nature.
Thus he finds the true fruit of virtue.

38
Virtue

Beaulac

Highest virtue is not concerned with being virtuous and thus is true virtue.
Low virtue cannot let go of being virtuous and thus is false virtue.

A person of high virtue does not act on things, and is also free of intention.
A person of high benevolence does act, but without the intent of action.
A very righteous person acts with intent.
A rigidly ritualistic person acts, and if there's no response, rolls up his sleeves and forces it on people.

So, when the Way is lost, "being virtuous" arises.
This kind of virtue fails, so we resort to rules of benevolence.
This kind of benevolence fails, so we turn to righteousness.
When righteousness is lost, rules of ritualized conduct arise.
> Truly, rules and rituals are the
> thin dead husk of sincerity and
> good faith
> and the beginning of trouble and
> confusion.
> Ritual augury is concerned with
> the Dao's flower,
> but is the beginning of
> foolishness.

That is why the great person:
> stays with the substantial rather
> than the superficial,
> prefers the fruit to the flower,
> and rejects "that out there" to
> hold to "this in here."

Comments

☯ The first of two consecutive verses which are the longest in the Tao Te Ching, followed immediately by the shortest (verse 40).

☯ "The master lives without rules and follows only his own true nature" (Martin 2). Living without rules can sound troublesome (and dangerous?), but I believe the implication is that the master does not need to be saddled with rules to be virtuous, as it is wholly a part of—and inseparable from—his true nature.

☯ When it comes to Virtue, I *highly recommend* Beaulac's section on Virtue (*De/Te*) in the back of his book, p. 151. One of the most enlightening I've seen, especially as it addresses the Taoist slant on the word.

39
Harmony

Mitchell

In harmony with the Tao,
the sky is clear and spacious,
the earth is solid and full,
all creatures flourish together,
content with the way they are,
endlessly repeating themselves,
endlessly renewed.

When man interferes with the Tao,
the sky becomes filthy,
the earth becomes depleted,
the equilibrium crumbles,
creatures become extinct.

The Master views the parts with
    compassion,
because he understands the whole.
His constant practice is humility.
He doesn't glitter like a jewel
but lets himself be shaped by the
    Tao,
as rugged and common as a stone.

39
Harmony

Martin

With this practice we find clarity.
Our horizons become expansive.
Our daily life becomes tranquil.
Our souls become inspired.
Our relationships become filled
with trust and honesty.
Our society flourishes.
Everything around us becomes
filled with creative life.

Without this practice we continue to
    suffer.
Our horizons contract.
Our daily life fills with anxiety.
Our souls wither.
Our relationships crumble.
Our society flounders.
Everything around us seems
    exhausted.

Despite our seeming prestige and
    power,
we know that we are really little
    children,
dependent on the Tao and helpless
    without it.

A wagon rolls along and does its job
with no fanfare at all.
Rather than clattering about
trying to be noticed,
we just roll along
like common stones in the river.

39
Harmony

Beaulac

Of ancient things that attained oneness:
    the heavens became one and thus
      clear,
    the Earth became one and thus firm,
    spirits became one and thus
      energized,
    empty valleys became one and thus
      filled with lushness,
    rulers became one and thus lead
      purely.
But, having reached oneness:
    if the heavens were ceaselessly
      clearing, they would rend;
    if the earth were always
      becoming firmer, it would
      crumble;
    if spirits were perpetually
      energetic, they would fizzle out;
    if valleys were always in growth,
      they would dry out;
    if rulers are honored and exalted
      without limit, they fall.

So then, honor has roots in humility, and the exalted need the foundation of lowliness. Hence, the custom of rulers calling themselves "the Orphaned One," "the Widowed One," and "the Unworthy One." Isn't this being rooted in humility?

Therefore they regard their many carriages the same as having no carriage.

Rather that tinkling and gleaming like jade they prefer to be solid as common rock.

Comments

☯ Besides re-stressing the ideas of oneness and Harmony, this verse also seems to be a lesson in humility. ("Rather than . . . trying to be noticed, we just roll along like common stones in the river." —Martin)

☯ Mitchell's rendition of the second stanza certainly graphically and sadly reminds us that our misplaced belief that we can *control* our environment has woefully failed us (and the environment) for years now, doesn't it?

40
Return

Mabry

Returning is the movement of the
    Tao.
Yielding is the way of the Tao.
All things in the world are born of
    existence.
Existence is born of non-existence.

40
Return

Martin

Following this path
returns us to our root.
It is a tender and gentle path.

Everything in the cosmos
depends on everything else.
Even our experience of life
depends upon our death.

40
Return

Beaulac

The universal Way progresses by
    returning.
The universal Way accomplishes by
    yielding.
All below Heaven arise out of being,
but being arises from Emptiness!

Comments

☯ The theme of Return keeps returning. This time it shows up in the Tao Te Ching's shortest verse.

☯ The *yielding* spoken of here does not carry any negative connotations of weakness. Instead it appears to be more of a yielding *into* the Way, which is more of a *letting go* of the desire to control, as mentioned in other verses.

☯ Mitchell translates the last line as "Being is born of non-being," and then notes in his comments: "'Non-being' means beyond the categories of being and non-being."

☯ Mitchell's first comment above seems to imply that *duality* comes from *unity* (where else, I suppose?) and, if so, would be a nice preview of verse 42, which expresses the same thoughts.

41
Laughable

Beaulac

A superior person hears of the Dao
  and diligently practices it.
An average person hears of the Dao
  and is sometimes aware, sometimes
  lost.
An inferior person hears of the Dao
  and laughs out loud.
If it isn't laughable, it isn't the Dao.
After all, it's the Dao which has
given rise to these maxims:
  The luminous way appears dull,
  the way that leads forward seems
    to retreat,
  the smooth way seems rough,
  the highest virtue seems low and
    empty as a valley,
  great purity seems sullied,
  abundant virtue seems deficient,
  steadfast virtue seems flimsy,
  simple truth seems uncertain.
  It's like a great square that has no
    corners,
  A great tool that does nothing,
  A great melody that has no
    sound,
  A great image that has no shape!
The Way is always here, hidden in
the background, nameless, creating
perfectly and completing perfectly.

41
Laughable

Martin 2

There seem to be three responses to
    the Tao:
Some hear of it and know in their
    souls that it is true.
They devote their lives to knowing it
    more fully.
Some hear of it and say, "that sounds
    interesting"
and think about it now and then.
Some hear of it and say, "Absurd!
    Airy-fairy nonsense!"
and laugh out loud.
This is why we have these adages:
Great wisdom seems childlike;
Great power seems weak;
True goodness seems suspect;
Great art seems ordinary and plain;
Great love seems uncaring;
Even Truth itself seems false.

41
Laughable

Hogan

When a wise person hears about Tao,
    he gets right with it.
When an ordinary person hears about
    Tao,
he tries to get right with it, but
    eventually gives up.
When a fool hears about Tao, he just
    laughs and laughs.
If he didn't laugh, it wouldn't be
    Tao.

Here's what they find so funny:
The path to enlightenment seems
    covered in shadows.
The way forward feels like taking a
    step back.
The easiest path seems difficult.
Those with the most virtue seem
    debased.
Those who are most pure seem to be
    grubby and soiled.
The deepest thoughts appear shallow.
The greatest strength looks like
    weakness.
What is most real strikes us as
    imaginary.
The largest space has no boundaries.
The greatest talent seems to produce
    nothing.
The greatest voice is unhearable.
The greatest beauty is invisible.

Tao is hidden to us and it has no
    name.
It is the source and the strength of all
    things.

Comments

☯ This is one of my favorite verses, primarily for the classic, almost-appropriately-humorous tidbit "If he didn't laugh, it wouldn't be Tao."!

☯ Beaulac's use of the words "After all . . ." following his version of the line ("If it isn't laughable, it isn't the Dao.") are most helpful in providing a bridge between those opening lines and the mini-paradoxes that follow, most obviously in Beaulac.

☯ Hogan's rendition also bridges the gap nicely, I think. (And so does the note in Martin 2, for that matter.) Not all translations succeed on that score.

☯ Beaulac's next-to-last line says "The Way is always here, hidden in the background . . ." I would be tempted to substitute "in plain sight" for "in the background."

42

Yin-Yang

Beaulac

Dao gives birth to the One,
the One gives birth to the two,
the Two gives birth to three,
and three gives birth to all the myriad
    things.
The myriad things carry *yin* at their
    backs and *yang* in their embrace;
being centered between these two
    energies produces harmony.

The world despises the orphaned, the
    desolate, and the unworthy,
and yet these are the names rulers use
    to refer to themselves.
Sometimes things gain by losing or
    lose by gaining.
What others have taught I also teach,
    namely this:
Those who live by force and
    aggression die by the same.
I see this as foundational.

42

Yin-Yang

Martin

Hidden in the mystery of the Tao
lies the original unity.
This unity contains the duality
of yin and yang.
Yin and yang together
produce the energy of creation
and give rise to all things.

Every atom of the cosmos
contains the yin and the yang
    together.
We feel this harmonious process
in the rising and falling
of our breath.

It seems natural to avoid loss and
    seek gain,
but on this path such distinctions are
    not helpful.
There is no gain without loss.
There is no fullness without
    deprivation.
Who knows how or when
one gives way to the other.
So we remain at the center
and trust events instead of forcing
    them.
This is the heart of all spiritual paths.

42
Yin-Yang

Bynner

Life, when it came to be,
Bore one, then two, then three
Elements of things;
And thus the three began
—Heaven and earth and man—
To balance happenings:
Cool night behind, warm day ahead,
For the living, for the dead.
Though a commoner be loth to say
That he is only common clay,
Kings and princes often state
How humbly they are leading,
Because in true succeeding
High and low correlate.
It is an ancient thought,
Which many men have taught,
That he who over-reaches
And tries to live by force
Shall die thereby of course,
And is what my own heart teaches.

Comments

☯ Another frequent Tao Te Ching topic: Seeking (as Beaulac phrases it in his notes) "the proper harmony between power and yielding, or gain and loss, rather than asserting one over the other." This is the essence of duality and Yin-Yang.

☯ Martin here seems to do a good job of blending the verse's topics that can otherwise seem disparate and somewhat disjoint.

☯ And Bynner's use of poetry is a nice touch, without distracting from the message.

Non-action

Mabry

The softest thing in the World
Overcomes the hardest thing in the
    World.
That which is without substance can
    enter
even where there is no space.

Therefore I know the value of
    non-action.

Teaching without words
And benefit without actions
There are few in the World who can
    grasp it.

Non-action

Martin 2

A fluid and gentle power
will overcome a stiff and inflexible
    strength.
A spacious vessel is more potent and
    creative
than one that is full to the brim.
This is why we work with wu-wei,
    "effortless action."
We act from stillness.
We talk from silence.
In a world of clamor and aggression,
this is not a popular way,
yet it is the only way to happiness.

43
Non-action

Feng & English

The softest thing in the universe
Overcomes the hardest thing in the
    universe.
That without substance can enter
    where there is no room.
Hence I know the value of
    non-action.

Teaching without words and work
    without doing
Are understood by very few.

Comments

☯ This verse is perhaps the poster child for the Taoist idea of *wu-wei.* The very essence of *go with the flow,* especially with the water images.

☯ A comment from my notes for which I can no longer find attribution: "Stay at the center, and trust events." Such a fiendishly simple concept—and yet, as Mabry says (and most translators echo), "few in the World . . . can grasp it." Or at least embody it. (Similar themes from verses 37 and 70.)

☯ For my own part, I am definitely *not* among the few in the world mentioned above! I can grasp the idea mentally, but putting it into practice remains deviously and frustratingly difficult for this particular Tao student. Perhaps the apparent irony is that I must try too hard?!

44
Contentment

Mabry

Fame or self: which is more
  important?

Your possessions or your person:
  which is worth more to you?

  Gain or loss: which is worse?

Therefore, to be obsessed with
  "things" is a great waste,
The more you gain, the greater your
  loss.

  Being content with what you
    have been given,
  You can avoid disgrace.
  Knowing when to stop,
  You will avoid danger.
  That way you can live a long and
    happy life.

44
Contentment

Feng & English

Fame or self: Which matters more?
Self or wealth: Which is more
  precious?
Gain or loss: Which is more painful?

He who is attached to things will
  suffer much.
He who saves will suffer heavy loss.
A contented man is never
  disappointed.
He who knows when to stop does not
  find himself in trouble.
He will stay forever safe.

44
Contentment

Martin 2

How others perceive you is of no
    concern.
How much wealth you have is of no
    concern.
These cause more suffering than
    happiness.
When your contentment springs from
    the fountain within you,
you will not be caught
by the traps of culture.
Your life will be blessed.

Comments

☻ In most translations, the opening questions of the verse, perhaps designed to provoke self-awareness, are phrased in varying manners, but they all seem, in *their very asking*, to suggest the answers. Martin 2 doesn't even bother to ask.

☻ Mitchell's note brings an interesting bit of perspective to these opening "*x* or *y*?" questions. He comments, "But why be caught in those dichotomies? . . . the Master accepts whatever comes to him. If fame comes, he uses it with integrity. If money comes, he uses it as pure energy. Success and failure are equally irrelevant to him, because his heart rests in the Tao."

☻ The message here seems clear and is reflected in the title: Contentment (though Non-attachment might also work). A contented man is never disappointed. "Know satisfaction" (Mair 7), but know when to stop. BE content. Or, we saw in Martin's opening line of verse 22, "Accepting what is, we find it to be perfect."

45
Perfection

Mitchell

True perfection seems imperfect,
yet it is perfectly itself.
True fullness seems empty,
yet it is fully present.

True straightness seems crooked.
True wisdom seems foolish.
True art seems artless.

The Master allows things to happen.
She shapes events as they come.
She steps out of the way
and lets the Tao speak for itself.

45
Perfection

Martin 2

So much of what we see around us
   seems flawed,
imperfect, and distorted.
But how can the Tao,
the essence of all forms,
be imperfect?
We want it to be direct,
but it winds around and about.
We want it to be clear,
but it seems confusing.
We want it to speak,
but it keeps silence.
So what are we to do?
Breathe in and out
as the trees and mountains breathe.
Be simply who you are
and nothing more is needed.

45
Perfection

Mair 8

Great perfection appears defective,
    but its usefulness is not
        diminished.
Great fullness appears empty,
    but its usefulness is not impaired.

Great straightness seems crooked,
Great cleverness seems clumsy,
Great triumph seems awkward.

Bustling about vanquishes cold,
Standing still vanquishes heat.

Pure and still,
    one can put things right
        everywhere under heaven.

Comments

☯ I am reminded (yet again!) of Martin's first line in verse 22, "Accepting what is, we find it to be perfect."

☯ Along those lines, I always smile at Mitchell's comment in his perceptive note on the verse: *True perfection*: A cracked coffee cup. The sound of traffic outside your window."

☯ In Martin 2's post-verse comment, he notes, "The idea that things are 'perfect' as they are does not mean we do not act in ways that seem to be 'improvements.'"

☯ I've always been puzzled by out-of-the-blue comments about heat/cold in most translations (seen here in Mair), despite some various explanations that exist. Viewing these as appropriate reactions (*à la* Martin 2's above) to the perfection of the changing weather seems to make sense to me. I doubt if that's what "the Old Boy" (see Further Comments) meant, but it helps me.

☯ Does anyone else view the first two sentences of the last stanza in Mitchell as *somewhat* contradictory (at least on the surface)—or at least more food for thought?

46
Enough

Mabry

When the World keeps to the Tao
Strong horses are best used to
    manufacture manure.
When the World forgets the Tao
War horses are bred outside the city.

There is no greater curse than
    discontent.
Nothing breeds trouble like greed.
Only one who is content with what is
    enough
will be content always.

46
Enough

Feng & English

When the Tao is present in the
    universe,
The horses haul manure.
When the Tao is absent from the
    universe,
War horses are bred outside the city.

There is no greater sin than desire,
No greater curse than discontent,
No greater misfortune than wanting
    something for oneself.
Therefore he who knows that enough
    is enough will always have
    enough.

46
Enough

Bynner

In a land where the way of life is
    understood
Race-horses are led back to serve the
    field;
In a land where the way of life is not
    understood
War-horses are bred on the autumn
    yield.
Owning is the entanglement,
Wanting is the bewilderment,
Taking is the presentiment:
Only he who contains content
Remains content.

Comments

☯ Most translators (and certainly the three here) make the verse's focus on being content and knowing when Enough is Enough. This reinforces the contentment theme in verse 44, just two verses earlier, and it speaks to me. But, then I also feel an apparent disconnect between the verse's two stanzas.

☯ Mitchell, however, helps me in this regard. His version (not included) looks a little deeper and changes the focus to fear ("no greater illusion than fear . . . no greater misfortune than having an enemy"; "whoever can see through all fear will always be safe"), and I believe there is wisdom and some helpful clarity there. For one thing, aren't we often told that the cause of *dis*content is fear? Further, focusing on fear makes a more reasonable transition in the first stanza.

☯ Also along those lines, Breed actually titles his rendition of this verse "fear" and does a nice job of tying these elements together.

47

Inner

Beaulac

Without stepping out the door,
you can know the whole cosmos.
Without looking out the window,
you can see Heaven's course.
The further one strays,
the less one knows.

So, the sage doesn't go elsewhere in
     order to know,
doesn't look elsewhere in order to
     understand,
and doesn't strive in order to
     accomplish.

47

Inner

Martin

It is not necessary to travel
to understand the world.
It is not necessary to look out the
     window
to see into ourselves.

The more we look outside ourselves
     for knowledge,
the less we know about anything.

We do not wander about
yet still we gain knowledge.
We do not look about
yet still we gain understanding.
We do not strive
yet still we accomplish everything.

47
Inner

Bynner

There is no need to run outside
For better seeing,
Nor to peer from a window. Rather
   abide
At the center of your being;
For the more you leave it, the less
   you learn.
Search your heart and see
If he is wise who takes each turn:
The way to do is to be.

Comments

☯ This is another one of a few verses (see also verses 26 and 80) that collectively lead to what I believe to be a misinterpretation of the Tao Te Ching, namely that it is anti-travel. It is true that, as Beaulac says, "Without stepping out the door, you can know the whole cosmos." But that does not mean one should not step outside the door!

☯ We can know the whole cosmos because we are part of it—and vice versa. (I call these "not one, not two" situations. See Further Comments for elaboration.) We can "understand the world" (Martin) because that knowledge comes from our Inner selves. And it's further true that, in Bynner's words, "the more you leave it [the center of your being], the less you learn." You can't travel somewhere *else* in order to find the center of your being.

☯ So, in my mind, the issue is not one of geography. The key is *what* you seek, acknowledge, become aware of, and carry with you, and not *where* you may or may not choose to travel.

48
Mastery

Mabry

To pursue learning is to grow a little
  more every day.
To pursue the Tao is to desire a little
  less every day.
    Desire less and less
    Until you arrive at "not-doing."
When you practice "not-doing,"
  nothing is left undone.

If you want to have the whole world,
  have nothing.
If you are always busy doing
  something,
you cannot enjoy the world.

48
Mastery

Martin 2

Information is not wisdom.
The more information we gain,
the more we assume we know.
The more we assume we know,
the less we see clearly.
In the practice of the Tao,
we rely less and less on what is
    called,
"information," and more and more on
    knowing "nothing;"
until at last we cease our fruitless
    efforts at the illusion of control,
and things unfold according to their
    nature.
Ourselves included.

48
Mastery

Hogan

Usually, we try to learn something
new every day.

But if we want to get right with Tao,
we have to let go of something every
day.

We do less and less, until we end up
doing nothing.
And it's when we do nothing that we
get the job done.

Let events take their course,
and everything will turn out in your
favor.
If you act on your ambitions, they
will never pan out.

Comments

☯ Another verse in the *wu-wei* hymn, not to mention the related *let go* and *simplicity* themes.

☯ There is an interesting comment in Mitchell on Mastery being something that can't be gained: "True mastery *is* letting things take their course." Nice insight.

☯ Perhaps this is obvious, but the more I read this verse, the more I am reassured (or convicted?) that we seek simplicity not *just* in things, lifestyles, and so on, but also in the more nebulous realms of ideas, assumptions, ambitions, opinions, and the like. This can be particularly tough spiritual work.

49
Transparent

Mabry

The Sage's heart is not set in stone.
She is as sensitive to the people's
    feelings as to her own.

She says, "To people who are good, I
    am good.
And to people who are not good?
I am good to them, too."
This is true goodness.

"People who are trustworthy, I trust.
And people who are not trustworthy,
    I also trust."
This is real trust.

The Sage who leads harmoniously
    considers the mind of
her people as well as her own.
They look to her anxiously.
They are like her own children.

49
Transparent

Martin

We hold no fixed opinions.
Our hearts are therefore open
to the hearts of all.

We extend kindness to the kind
and unkind alike.
Thus kindness becomes our very
    nature.

We extend trust to the trustworthy
and untrustworthy alike.
Thus trust becomes our very nature.

We don't contend with people
by seeking to gain advantage.
People around us lose their edge
and we become loving friends
to the whole world.

49
Transparent

Mair 12

The sage never has a mind of his
    own;
He considers the minds of the
    common people to be his mind.

Treat well those who are good,
Also treat well those who are not
    good;
        thus is goodness attained.

Be sincere to those who are sincere,
Also be sincere to those who are
    insincere;
        thus is sincerity attained.

The sage
    is self-effacing in his dealings
        with all under heaven,
        and bemuddles his mind for the
            sake of all under heaven.

The common people all rivet their
    eyes and ears upon him,
And the sage makes them all chuckle
    like children.

Comments

☻ In his notes, Beaulac writes, "In this verse we see the effect of the sage's inner state on the outer realm." This strikes me as nicely said and a good overview.

☻ It is in that spirit that the title Transparent has been chosen. The sage is not complex, not distracted by outer input (and in that sense the eyes/ears are covered), but as his/her goodness, trust, and the like are seen and shared, they spread and perpetuate.

☻ As might be expected, there are interesting variations of the middle stanzas. For those stanzas only, Mair switches to second person (technically imperative here), and Feng & English use first person. (Mabry also does this, but in the context of quoting the sage.)

50
Life

Bynner

Death might appear to be the issue of
    life,
Since for every three out of ten being
    born
Three out of ten are dying.
Then why
Should another three out of ten
    continue breeding death?
Because of sheer madness to
    multiply.
But there is one out of ten, they say,
    so sure of life
That tiger and wild bull keep clear of
    his inland path,
Weapons turn from him on the
    battle-field,
No bull-horn could tell where to gore
    him,
No tiger-claw where to tear him,
No weapon where to enter him.
And why?
Because he has no death to die.

50
Life

Martin 2

Some people think only of life and
    ignore death.
Some think only of death, and ignore
    life.
Some don't think about either life or
    death.
Whatever they think,
they all die in the end.
The follower of the Tao knows death
    will come,
therefore knows how to live:
without illusions; without fear;
without resistance; and without
    suffering.
Neither life nor death can disturb this
    one.

50
Life

Hogan

People who look for the secret of
   long life wind up dead.

Their bodies are the focus of their
   lives and the source of their
   death,
because they think a healthy body is
   all there is to life.

Lao Tzu used to say a man who truly
   understood life
could walk through the jungle
   without fear
or across a battlefield without armor,
   totally unarmed.
Wild animals and weapons couldn't
   kill him.

I know, I know: What's that
   supposed to mean?
"Well, he couldn't be killed," Lao
   Tzu said,
"because his body wasn't where he
   kept his death."

Comments

☻ If there is a passage in the Tao Te Ching for which there is no traditional translation, or even clear agreement on the message, it must be this one. It's almost ironic that what I call "ye olde 3 in 10 classic" has three different strands of thought about its translation and its meanings. And further variations, of course, within each of those camps.

☻ Very briefly: (a) there are some who translate the three-in-ten less literally, as one third, and discuss three patterns of living; (b) others (but fewer) stay literal with the three in ten, leaving one person (the sage?) in ten who *gets it right*, so to speak; (c) there is a smaller-but-still-significant group who translates (with solid reasoning) three in ten as *thirteen* and refer then to that number in at least three (!) different ways, usually centering on body openings.

☻ There is an excellent summary of the above situation, including alternate, sensible translations, in Beaulac's post-verse note. This is really-shouldn't-miss information, but too long to fairly summarize here (or even quote in Further Comments).

51

Expression

Breed

The Tao gives birth to every creature
in the universe.
Its outflowing nourishes everything.
Each thing receives its shape
according to its nature.
Each becomes complete in harmony
with its circumstances.
This is why the entire universe,
without exception,
expresses the Tao.
All things reveal its creative stream.
This expression is completely
natural,
a spontaneous tribute.
In this way, the Tao births all things,
nourishes them, brings them to their
full growth,
cares for them lovingly, completes
them, matures them,
maintains them, and overspreads
them.
It births them and makes no claim.
It quietly and humbly carries them
through each step of their existence.
This is the mystery of the Tao.

51

Expression

Martin 2

Giving honor to the Tao is not a duty.
Neither is it a test of loyalty
nor a commandment from on high.
Every form in all the Cosmos
delights in the Tao
and gives it honor in the simple act of
being.
The Tao does not demand
or expect anything from us.
It guides us without controlling.
It nurtures us without owning us.
We are all expressions
of this Formless Mystery,
nurtured, sustained,
and finally returned to our Origin.

51
Expression

Feng & English

All things arise from Tao.
They are nourished by Virtue.
They are formed from matter.
They are shaped by environment.
Thus the ten thousand things all
    respect Tao and honor Virtue.
Respect of Tao and honor of Virtue
    are not demanded,
But they are in the nature of things.

Therefore all things arise from Tao.
By Virtue they are nourished,
Developed, cared for,
Sheltered, comforted,
Grown, and protected.
Creating without claiming,
Doing without taking credit,
Guiding without interfering,
This is Primal Virtue.

Comments

☯ Most translations—with considerable variations, of course, speak of all beings (or "the ten thousand things") arising from the Tao and then honoring or respecting it (the Tao) as part of their nature.

☯ Even understanding that this *honoring* is nowhere close to *worship*, in any traditional sense, I often struggle with these thoughts. I think I get hung up on whether the honoring is conscious or not.

☯ But when I see the verb translated as *expressing* the Tao (*à la* Breed here, and others), the confusion instantly drops away for me. Our very life is an *Expression* of the Tao; hence we *honor* it—consciously or otherwise— by our very existence.

☯ All of this is further tied into the idea of virtue ("By Virtue they are nourished" in Feng & English). The Taoist meaning in these contexts seems to be much closer to Expression, but I think it is obscured by our own connotations of virtue as goodness.

☯ For a comparison of some of the various ways the final line (involving virtue) is translated, see the Further Comments.

52
Senses

Mabry

The World has an origin
Which we may regard as the Mother
  of the Universe.
Knowing the Mother, we can also
  come to know
her children.
Knowing the children, return and
  hold fast to the Mother.
Doing this, you will not meet with
  danger
your whole life long.

    Close your mouth
    Go easy on the senses
    And life will not be so hard.

    If you spend your life filling your
      senses
    And rushing around "doing"
      things
    You will be beyond hope.

To concern yourself with the
  beautiful and small
is true wisdom.
To foster gentleness is true strength.
Choose to do what is wise and return
  to wisdom.
Then you will avoid life's troubles.
This is called practicing consistency.

52
Senses

Martin 2

Since the Tao gave birth to the
  Cosmos,
she can truly be called, "Mother."
Everything we see around us
may be called Her children.
If we recognize Her children,
we recognize Her,
for She and Her children are One.
A child at rest in his mother's arms
  has no desires, no fears,
and no judgments in his mind.
If we sit very still
and let our mind become quiet,
we will discover that we are just like
  this child.
If we scurry about, voicing our
  opinions
and focusing on our fears, we will
  live in chaos.
Contentment is our normal state.
We are tender hearted by nature,
and we know that deep within our
  souls,
we are enlightened and at peace.

Beaulac

All below Heaven have a beginning
which may be called the Mother of
    the world.
When you come to know the Mother,
you can then recognize the children.
Having properly recognized the
    children,
you can return to abiding in the
    Mother,
and remain free of harm.

Close the mouth and shut the gates,
and throughout life you will avoid
    exhaustion.
As long as your mouth is going and
    you are busy about everything,
you remain beyond rescue.

To discern the small and subtle is
    illumination.
To remain gentle is strength.
When you follow light back to the
    source of illumination,
you don't get lost or suffer
    destruction.
You can call this "following the
    Eternal."

Comments

☻ See similar thoughts in verse 12 (the *five senses* verse) and the comments there.

☻ Some commentators consider the 1st stanza a continuation of verse 51.

☻ The wording in the 2nd stanza (indented in Mabry) of most translations is quite similar to wordings in both verses 4 and 56. See comment on verse 4.

☻ See Further Comments for a summary of some authors' choices for the last line.

☻ Martin 2's note seems to verbalize the impression I get from this verse: "The connecting thread [of the various themes] seems to be that the mysterious origin, the Mother Tao, and the ordinary things of life are part of the same thing. To *truly know* the ordinary thing, the ordinary moment, is to know the mysterious Tao." (Italics mine.)

☻ And, further, therefore, the more we can identify with the mysterious origin (with the help of the ordinary things), the more we become safe from (the illusion of) harm.

Sidetracked

Feng & English

If I have even just a little sense,
I will walk on the main road and my
    only fear will be of straying from
    it.
Keeping to the main road is easy,
But people love to be sidetracked.

When the court is arrayed in
    splendor,
The fields are full of weeds,
And the granaries are bare.
Some wear gorgeous clothes,
Carry sharp swords,
And indulge themselves with food
    and drink;
They have more possessions than
    they can use.
They are robber barons.
This is certainly not the way of Tao.

53

Sidetracked

Martin 2

I would love to follow the Tao every
    moment of my life,
but distractions are everywhere,
and everyone is pushing, pulling,
    wanting my attention.
The rich buy every kind of toy for
    their amusement.
The government buys every kind of
    weapon for their protection.
A few drink fine wine and eat at
    tables
laden with the finest meats.
All this goes on at the expense
of the mass of ordinary people,
    whose fields grow money
and whose jobs make money for the
    very few.
This is contrary to the flow of the
    Tao
and will surely end in misery.

53
Sidetracked

Hogan

If I had any sense, I'd be trying to get
   right with Tao,
and the only thing I'd worry about
   would be messing up.
It's not that hard to get right with
   Tao,
but people are easily distracted.

"When the king's palace is full of
   treasure,"
Lao Tzu said, "ordinary people's
   fields
are smothered with weeds, and the
   food supplies run out."

Today, you see sharply dressed
   people
carrying flashy weapons and living
   the high life.

They own more than they could ever
   use, let alone need.

They're nothing but gangsters and
   crooks.
That's not what Tao's about.

Comments

☻ Lines similar to the leading sentence used here by Feng & English and Hogan are omitted in some translations (Mitchell, for example), which lead instead with "Keeping to the Way is easy" or the rough equivalent.

☻ Martin 2's note reminds us that Lao Tzu was considered a revolutionary by the leaders in his time. And this can account for the scolding nature in the second half of the verse, which can be felt more in some renditions than others.

☻ The tendency of most of us to get Sidetracked from the "easy" (?!) way of the Tao leads to the choice for the title for this verse.

☻ See Further Comments for an interesting note from Mair about a Chinese pun which is used in the last line, and references to a similar situation in the Bhagavad Gita.

54
Rooted

Mitchell

Whoever is planted in the Tao
will not be rooted up.
Whoever embraces the Tao
will not slip away.
Her name will be held in honor
from generation to generation.

Let the Tao be present in your life
and you will become genuine.
Let it be present in your family
and your family will flourish.
Let it be present in your country
and your country will be an example
to all countries in the world.
Let it be present in the universe
and the universe will sing.

How do I know this is true?
By looking inside myself.

54
Rooted

Martin

If we establish ourselves on this path,
we will not be shaken by events.
If we take it into our hearts,
our children and their children will
    benefit.

This path returns us to our true self.
It brings our families abundant joy.
It brings our communities a lasting
    legacy.
It brings our countries true
    prosperity.

All that is expresses this path.
Therefore we practice awareness
in each and every moment.
We see ourselves in every person
    we meet.
The whole world becomes our
    family,
our community,
our country.

How do we make this discovery?
By sitting still and looking within.

54
Rooted

Breed

That which is planted by the Tao
can never be unrooted.
That which the Tao enfolds,
will never be destroyed.
Endless generations will honor
what has been accomplished.
If you nurture the Tao within you,
you will have both vigor and
integrity.
Your family will be enriched.
Your community will thrive.
Your entire nation will prosper.
Observe how the Tao affects each
level:
the individual, the family,
the community, the nation.
How do I know this is true?
By observation.

Comments

☯ Some of the thoughts in this verse are reminiscent of parts of verse 51 (Expression) (see for example Martin's line, "All that is expresses this path.") and verse 26 (Grounded).

☯ And see verse 26 for related thoughts about being Rooted, or grounded, in the Tao.

☯ Mitchell's 2nd stanza speaks to me, partly due to his use of the word *let*. Somehow, the idea of trying to *cultivate* or grow the Tao within ourselves is not as freeing for me as remembering it's already there and *letting* it be present.

55
Vitality

Mitchell

He who is in harmony with the Tao
is like a newborn child.
Its bones are soft, its muscles are
    weak,
but its grip is powerful.
It doesn't know about the union
of male and female,
yet its penis can stand erect,
so intense is its vital power.
It can scream its head off all day,
yet it never becomes hoarse,
so complete is its harmony.

The Master's power is like this.
He lets all things come and go
effortlessly, without desire.
He never expects results;
thus he is never disappointed.
He is never disappointed;
thus his spirit never grows old.

55
Vitality

Martin 2

Harmony with the Tao brings a life
    of innocent ease.
Like a baby who has not yet learned
    to stiffen against life;
whose body is soft, but whose spirit
    is powerful;
who resists nothing, but conquers
    everything;
who doesn't yet see himself as
    separate from the Tao.
To know this harmony is to live
    effortlessly in the present
    moment,
without strain, aggression, or force;
and to experience lasting peace.
Strain, aggression, and force are
    contrary to the Tao
and their results will not last.

55
Vitality

Legge

He who has in himself abundantly the attributes (of the Tao) is like an infant. Poisonous insects will not sting him; fierce beasts will not seize him; birds of prey will not strike him.

(The infant's) bones are weak and its sinews soft, but yet its grasp is firm. It knows not yet the union of male and female, and yet its virile member may be excited;—showing the perfection of its physical essence. All day long it will cry without its throat becoming hoarse;—showing the harmony (in its constitution).

To him by whom this harmony is
    known,
(The secret of) the unchanging (Tao)
    is shown,
And in the knowledge wisdom finds
    its throne.
All life-increasing arts to evil turn;
Where the mind makes the vital
    breath to burn,
(False) is the strength,
    (and o'er it we should mourn.)

When things have become strong, they (then) become old, which may be said to be contrary to the Tao. Whatever is contrary to the Tao soon ends.

Comments

☻ I suspect, as we age, we all remember fondly that gift of youth's Vitality. Somehow this verse reminds me that harmony with life and the Tao can increase vitality (or at least slow its departure?).

☻ I like Martin 2's line "To know this harmony is to live effortlessly in the present moment." In his note, he goes on to say "To 'live effortlessly' is not to live without thinking or planning. It is to live without the resistance and strain of what S. Suzuki . . . called 'second thoughts,'" which he later describes as "rabbit trails of associative thinking" that follow our original thought. (Also called "monkey mind" by others.)

☻ I'm not at all convinced these are relevant thoughts (my own monkey mind at work?), but as I write this comment, for some reason, I'm reminded of two sayings (though both have multiple phrasings, as well as fuzzy and/or conflicting attributions—see Further Comments): (1) Too bad that youth has to be wasted on the young. (2) Man does not quit playing because he grows old. He grows old because he quits playing.

56
Union

Mabry

Those who know, do not speak.
Those who speak, do not know.

    So shut your mouth
    Guard your senses
    Blunt your sharpness
    Untangle your affairs
    Soften your glare
    Be one with all dust.
    This is the mystery of union.

You cannot approach it
Yet you cannot escape it.
You cannot benefit it
Yet you cannot harm it.
You cannot bestow any honor on it
Yet you cannot rob it of its dignity.
That is why the whole Universe
  reveres it.

56
Union

Beaulac

Those who know don't talk about it;
those who talk don't know.
    Close the mouth,
    shut the gates,
    soften the glare,
    join with the settling dust,
    blunt the sharp points,
    untangle the complications.
This is called the profound union.
In this union,
    there is no getting closer to or
     farther from,
    no gaining or losing
    no exalting or debasing.
And that's why nature honors it
  above all else.

56
Union

Breed

The person who truly knows the Tao
doesn't talk much about it;
the person who is always wanting to
talk about the Tao
doesn't really know much about it.
If you know the Tao,
you will keep your mouth shut
and guard your senses.
You will round off your sharp edges
and unravel your complexities.
You will shield your own light
and be content to walk in others'
shadows.
This is called the Mysterious
Harmony.
Here you can be treated neither too
familiarly
nor too distantly.
You are beyond all thought of either
your own profit
or your own injury.
You are concerned with neither
humility nor pride,
and yet you are equal to the person
with the highest position in the
world.

Comments

☯ The first line alone makes this another of the classics, and it may be one of the three or four most famous lines of the Tao (rivaling the first line of verse 1 and the classic translation "journey of a thousand miles" in verse 64?).

☯ I like Breed's slightly amplified version (see left) of the line, though I worry it applies to anyone compiling a book about Tao Te Ching translations. But since I don't claim to "truly know the Tao," perhaps I'm OK.

☯ Martin takes a slightly different tack in his note: "A good guideline for the depth of practice in our life is noticing whether or not we are trying to convert others to our point of view." Interesting—and thought provoking.

☯ Ellen Chen (1989, 188) remarks in her general comments on this verse, "We may regard the whole chapter as giving us the psychology of the Taoist ruler/mystic."

Living

Beaulac

Use straightforwardness to govern a
	state;
misdirection is for conducting
	battles.
Better yet, be empty of all such
	affairs and win the world!
How do I know this is indeed so?
By noticing this:
> the more restrictive the taboos,
> 	the poorer the people;
> the finer the weapons, the more
> 	troubled the State;
> the more ingenious the
> 	technology, the more bizarre
> 	things are made;
> the more issues become legal
> 	matters, the more people
> 	become criminals.

So, the sage says,
> I take no action, and the people
> 	transform themselves;
> I enjoy quietude, and the people
> 	correct themselves;
> I create no agendas, and the
> 	people prosper by themselves;
> I am free of attachments, and the
> 	people simplify their own lives.

Living

Martin

To guide a country
we use administrative skills.
To wage a war
we use surprise tactics.
But to gain joy in living
we let life live itself.

What does "let life live itself" mean?
The harder we try
the more our efforts fail.
The more we arm ourselves
the more chaos we experience.
The more schemes we plan
the less predictable are the results.
The more rules we impose
the more we become rule-breakers.

So in this practice
we stop trying to change ourselves
and find that we naturally change.
We stop trying to be good
and find that goodness is our nature.
We stop trying to get rich,
and find that our life is full of
	abundance.
We stop trying to get our own way
and find that we enjoy our life.

57
Living

Hogan

You can run a country by sticking to
    principles,
and you can win a war with strategy
    and tactics.
But you can gain the entire world by
    doing nothing at all.

How do I know this? I've seen it
    happen:
The more restrictions a nation
    imposes,
the poorer its people become.
When a nation hoards weapons,
troubles arise from within and from
    without.
When its leaders try to be cunning
    and clever,
the situation spins further out of
    control.
When they try to fix things by
    passing more laws,
they only increase the number of
    outlaws.

A wise leader says to himself:
"I do nothing, and people transform
    themselves.
I keep silent, and they do the right
    thing on their own.
I stay out of the way, and they
    prosper.
I want for nothing, and they lead
    simple lives."

Comments

☯ In most translations, this becomes a Taoist guide to good leadership and effective governance, and it is indeed a good one, even if increasingly divorced from the ways of these times.

☯ But even in those translations, as so often occurs, one begins to get an inkling that these governing principles work well for running our lives as well. (Hence the Living title.)

☯ Martin (as is his habit) quickly makes this broader theme the focus of his rendition ("We stop trying to change ourselves and find that we naturally change."), and I think, alongside good governance, it works well as the verse's main theme.

Example

Mitchell

If a country is governed with
    tolerance,
the people are comfortable and
    honest.
If a country is governed with
    repression,
the people are depressed and crafty.

When the will to power is in charge,
the higher the ideals, the lower the
    results.
Try to make people happy,
and you lay the groundwork for
    misery.
Try to make people moral,
and you lay the groundwork for
    vice.

Thus the Master is content
to serve as an example
and not to impose her will.
She is pointed, but doesn't pierce.
Straightforward, but supple.
Radiant, but easy on the eyes.

58

Example

Martin 2

When people interfere in the lives of
    others,
instead of each following their own
    path,
everyone remains restless,
    discontent, and fearful.
Trying to make others happy doesn't
    work,
because we can't know whether our
    actions
will bring benefit or harm.
Trying to make others behave
    doesn't work,
because we can't know their inner
    heart.
Yet our culture tries to function as if
we could actually do these things.
Be content to follow the Tao as you
    see it unfold before you.
Speak clearly of what you see,
but don't impose what you see on
    others.
Be a companion to people,
but don't dominate them.

58
Example

Beaulac

When the government is dulled
  and unobtrusive
people live simply and
  wholesomely.
Where the government is sharp
  and prying
people become restless and
  contentious.
Bad fortune rides on good
  fortune,
and good fortune is concealed in
  bad fortune
So, who knows which is the ultimate
  outcome?
There is no ordered norm.
What is "as it should be" turns into
  what "ought not to be,"
and what is meant for good becomes
  something sinister.
People have been confused for a long
  time.
  Therefore, the sage is a straight
    edge, but doesn't cut;
  is sharp, but doesn't stab;
  is straightforward, but not severe;
  is illuminating, but not blinding.

Comments

☯ Often seen as a continuation of verse 57, we see this verse leading with contrasting styles of government and their effects on the people. And, even more clearly than verse 57, it also turns this contrast into a similar comparison of the behavior of the sage, and the corresponding effects on his/her environment.

☯ Indeed, the sage/master is "content to serve as an example and not to impose her will" (Mitchell).

☯ Also present here is the warning that, just as an intrusive government can have disruptive outcomes, so too can what might be called over-aggressive attempts at improvement. As Beaulac points out, this can lead to what is "as it should be" turning into what "ought not to be." Who knows where our well-intentioned efforts might lead? "People have been confused" about this endlessly.

☯ So, this is another way that the sage/master/ruler can serve as an Example, helping to cut through this confusion by wisely being content to "follow the Tao as you see it unfold before you" (Martin 2).

☯ Is Martin 2's quote above more helpful if you read it as "the Tao as *you* see it unfold"?

59
Moderation

Mabry

In leading people and serving
    Heaven
There is nothing better than
    moderation.
In moderation, one is already
    following the Tao.
When one follows the Tao, great
    goodness is abundant.
When great goodness is in
    abundance,
There is nothing that cannot be
    overcome.
When there is nothing that cannot be
    overcome
Then there are no limits.
Having no limits, one can certainly
    govern a country.
If you know the country's Mother,
    you will long endure.

I call this having deep roots and a
    firm stalk.
This is the Way of long life and great
    insight.

59
Moderation

Martin

Moderation is the best way
to care for our affairs.
It frees us from fixed plans
that waste our power.
We never punish ourselves
for things we do or don't do,
so our power remains available.
With it we can respond
to the shifting winds of life
and use everything for good.

We are able to take care of our
    affairs,
no matter how complicated,
with the gentle ease
of a mother caring for her child.

Deeply rooted in our practice,
we never become confused
or lose our way.

59
Moderation

Beaulac

In governing people and attending to
    Heaven
there's nothing better than
    moderation.
In moderation one is yielding from
    the start.
"Yielding form the start" means
    abundant cultivation of virtue.
Abundant cultivation of virtue means
    anything can be overcome.
That anything can be overcome
    means knowing no limitations.
Knowing no limitations makes one
    fit to guard the country.
It is by guarding the country's
    Mother that one endures long.
This is called having deep roots and a
    sturdy trunk—
the way to long life and enduring
    vision.

Comments

❂ This verse could conceivably be called the Taoist description of the Buddhist *Middle Way*.

❂ I've always liked the progressions in this verse from the various equivalents of "no limits" through "governing a country" and "knowing the Mother."

❂ Beaulac translates *no limits* as an "abundant cultivation of virtue," and as previously mentioned, his section on virtue (p.151) is insightful and worth exploring.

❂ I can't help but be reminded, perhaps irreverently in this case, of the hidden wisdom in the familiar saying, "Moderation in all things, including moderation."

❂ For multiple translations of the "deep roots" line near the end of this verse, see Further Comments.

Accord

Breed

Governing a great realm is like
cooking small fish:
stir them and they break apart easily.
When the realm is governed
according to the Tao,
the evil from the past loses its
spiritual energy.
The energy is still there,
but it will no longer be used to hurt
others.
It still has the power to be
destructive,
but the ruler of the realm
has brought everything into unity and
peace.
The ruler works in harmony with the
past,
so that past and present converge for
good within the Tao.

Accord

Martin 2

If you keep poking the fish you're
frying,
you will ruin your dinner.
If you keep poking at your fears,
you will ruin your life.
Fear, greed, doubt, and restlessness
are the products of our mind.
If we prod and stir them,
they will permeate our thinking
and spread out into our lives.
If we let them come and go,
they will find no place to cling,
and they will fade away
and no longer run our lives.

60
Accord

Mair 23

Ruling a big kingdom is like
   cooking a small fish.
If one oversees all under heaven
   in accord with the Way,
      demons have no spirit.
It is not that the demons have no
   spirit,
      but that their spirits do not
         harm people.
It is not merely that their spirits
   do not harm people,
      but that the sage also does not
         harm them.

Now,
   When neither harms the other,
      integrity accrues to both.

Comments

☯ The famous "cooking a small fish" verse. What a helpful image for this theme.

☯ Another (of many) where substituting "living a life" for "governing a country" works equally well. And when we do that, *à la* Martin 2, the "cooking a small fish" or, as he puts it, "poking at [our] fears" really hits closer to home.

☯ Ah, if we could just internalize and manifest that "fear, greed, doubt, and restlessness are products of our mind" (Martin 2).

☯ Mair has an interesting note (23.3, 109) on his use of the word demons here. (Others often use *evil*.)

61
Yielding

Mabry

A great country is like a low-lying
  lake where many rivers converge;
A focal point for the Earth, the
  feminine Spirit of the World.
The female always overcomes the
  male by stillness.
Stillness is the lowest position.

  Therefore a big country,
  By placing itself below a smaller
    country
  Will win the smaller country.

  And a small country,
  By placing itself below a larger
    country
  Will gain the large country.

  Therefore, by being humble, one
    gains
  And the other, being humble
    already, also gains.

  A great country needs to embrace
    the lowly.
  The small country needs to serve
    others.
  Thus, both needs are satisfied
  And each gets what it wants.

Remember, the great country should
  always humble itself.

61
Yielding

Breed

A nation becomes great by being like
  a low-lying stream:
it becomes the center into which all
  the smaller streams flow.
Let me illustrate this from masculine-
  feminine interactions:
the feminine overcomes the
  masculine with her stillness.
You can think of stillness as a form
  of humility,
and yet by lowering yourself,
  you gain everything.
In this way, great power yields to
  weaker,
and gains the smaller power for
  itself,
while small powers yield to greater,
  and win favor.
The great power wishes only to unite
  and nourish others.
The smaller power wishes to serve
  and be protected.
Each gets what it wants.
But first the greater power must learn
  to be humble.

61
Yielding

Legge

What makes a great state is its being (like) a low-lying, down-flowing (stream);—it becomes the centre to which tend (all the small states) under heaven.

(To illustrate from) the case of all females:—the female always overcomes the male by her stillness. Stillness may be considered (a sort of) abasement.

Thus it is that a great state, by condescending to small states, gains them for itself; and that small states, by abasing themselves to a great state, win it over to them. In the one case the abasement leads to gaining adherents, in the other case to procuring favour.

The great state only wishes to unite men together and nourish them; a small state only wishes to be received by, and to serve, the other. Each gets what it desires, but the great state must learn to abase itself.

Comments

☯ This verse has always seemed like a tough nut to crack. Even with a variety of good translations, and a faint hint of where this is pointing, I've never felt comfortable trying to unravel it for myself.

☯ I feel somewhat better knowing I'm not alone here. Ellen Chen (1989, 196), starts her comments, "Contrary to the remarks of some commentators . . . this chapter is not on international intrigue but international peace and cooperation." (I'm not much moved by that view either.) And, even my frequent notes-go-to Needleman (F&E) remains quiet in his notes on this one.

☯ Legge's note makes an interesting point by comparing this verse's theme to the Bible's "He that humbleth himself shall be exalted" (Luke 14:11, KJV). I'm not sure the principle translates easily, but I think it could easily be a road map for individuals *as well as* countries.

62
Invaluable

Mabry

The Tao is the bosom of the Universe
It is the good person's treasure
And the bad person's refuge.

Flattery may buy one's position
And good deeds can win people over
But if one's heart is not pure
That is all the more reason to cling to
    the Tao!

Therefore when a king is coronated,
Crowned in ceremony,
Presented with gifts of rare value,
And escorted in luxury,
All these things pale when compared
    to the humble gift
of the Tao, offered in silence.

Why did the Sages of old value the
    Tao so much?
Because when you seek, you find
And when you sin, you are forgiven.

That is why the Tao is the greatest
    treasure of the Universe.

62
Invaluable

Martin

This path is the source of all that is.
It is the refuge of those who follow
    it.
It is the protector of those who ignore
    it.

We honor those
who show no interest in this path
with gentle words and
    loving-kindness.

Greater than any gift of wealth or
    power
is the quiet offering of ourselves to
    one another.
Two truths guide our practice:
"Look inside and you will find,"
and
"You are free of fault."

For this reason this path
is dear to us beyond all else.

62
Invaluable

Hogan

Every living thing gets its strength
from Tao.
Good people respect the value of
Tao.
The wicked and foolish don't, but
Tao provides for them anyway.

Some people gain power and prestige
through fancy words,
others through great deeds.
But Tao is available to everyone, not
just the powerful.
So don't look down on anybody.

When other people become powerful,
and everybody lines up to kiss their
asses,
sit still and stay right with Tao.

Why have the Masters always
respected Tao?
Because when you get right with
Tao,
you can always find what you need
to get by,
and trouble can never find you.

Comments

☯ I'll echo my thoughts in verse 27 (and its corresponding Further Comment) here. As often as the Tao Te Ching advises not to over-label or go too far with distinctions, verses like this that speak of the *good* or *bad* person always give me pause. I like the way Martin avoids these labels in his lines 2–5, for example.

☯ And I like the feel of Hogan's rendition here also (see left). His modern voice speaks to me, and I like the way his verse comes together.

☯ In Mitchell's wording of the 2nd stanza (not included here), he says "the Tao is beyond all value, and no one can achieve it." Perhaps I'm being pedantic, but I'm not sure the Tao itself is something that could be *achieved.* Any more than the atmosphere around us. It cannot be achieved because it is already ever-present, and as Hogan says, "available to everyone." See Further Comments for more thoughts about this stanza.

☯ Mair (25.15, 110) has an interesting note that suggests that the "seek . . . find" and "sin . . . forgiven" lines (see Mabry) are perhaps antecedents for similar lines in Matthew 7:7 and 7:8.

63
Attention

Mabry

Do without "doing."
Work without forcing.
Taste without seasonings.
Recognize the Great in the small,
And the many in the few.

Repay hatred with kindness.

Deal with the difficult while it is still
    easy.
Begin great works while they are
    small.
Certainly the Earth does difficult
    work with ease,
And accomplishes great affairs from
    small beginnings.
So, the Sage, by not striving for
    greatness,
Achieves greatness.

A person who makes promises
    lightly
Is not regarded as trustworthy.

If you think everything is easy,
You will find only difficulty.
That is why the Sage considers all
    things difficult
And finds nothing too difficult in the
    end.

63
Attention

Beaulac

Act without acting;
go about your business without
    busyness;
savor what is without flavor.
Great or small, many or few,
repay wrongs with kindness.
Plan for difficulties while they're still
    easy,
and deal with great matters while
    they're small.
Truly, the world's difficult affairs
    start out easy
and its great affairs start out small.
Therefore the sage never has to act in
    a big way to accomplish great
    things.
Agreeing too easily makes one
    untrustworthy,
and taking it too easy lets difficulties
    arise.
So, the sage is wary of difficulties
and thus avoids them altogether.

63
Attention

Legge

(It is the way of the Tao) to act without (thinking of) acting; to conduct affairs without (feeling the) trouble of them; to taste without discerning any flavour; to consider what is small as great, and a few as many; and to recompense injury with kindness.

(The master of it) anticipates things that are difficult while they are easy, and does things that would become great while they are small. All difficult things in the world are sure to arise from a previous state in which they were easy, and all great things from one in which they were small. Therefore the sage, while he never does what is great, is able on that account to accomplish the greatest things.

He who lightly promises is sure to keep but little faith; he who is continually thinking things easy is sure to find them difficult. Therefore the sage sees difficulty even in what seems easy, and so never has any difficulties.

Comments

☯ This verse is clearly a prelude to and partner of verse 64. Many, if not most, commentators view them as a pair—this despite the more classic nature of verse 64.

☯ Needleman's (F&E) note underscores this: "These two chapters deal with the art of living considered as the practice of giving one's best attention to the present moment with all its details." It is this excerpt that influenced the final decision on the title for this verse.

☯ See continued comments along these lines in verse 64.

64
Beginnings

Mabry

What is at rest is easy to maintain.
What has not yet happened is easy to
  plan.
That which is fragile is easily shattered
That which is tiny is easily scattered.

  Correct problems before they occur.
  Intervene before chaos erupts.

A tree too big around to hug is produced
  from a tiny sprout.
A nine-story tower begins with a mound
  of dirt.
A thousand-mile journey begins with
  your own two feet.

  Whoever tries will fail.
  Whoever clutches, loses.

  Therefore the Sage, not trying,
    cannot fail
  Not clutching, she cannot lose.

  When people try,
  they usually fail just on the brink of
    success.
  If one is as cautious at the outset as
    at the end,
  One cannot fail.

Therefore the Sage desires nothing so
  much
as to be desireless.
She does not value rare and expensive
  goods.
She unlearns what she was once taught
And helps the people regain what they
  have lost;
To help every being assume its natural
  way of being,
And not dare to force anything.

64
Beginnings

Martin 2

All trouble begins in the mind.
If we cultivate a mind that's still and
    calm,
spacious and open,
we can deal with trouble before it
    starts.
A tree grows naturally, without
    effort,
beginning with a tiny seedling.
A thousand mile journey is taken,
    without effort,
beginning with a single step.
So don't let a restless mind
lead you to aggressive action.
If you force events, you will fail.
Be patient.
Let your actions emerge from a quiet
    place.
In this way all beings will be blessed.

64
Beginnings

Beaulac

What is still peaceful is easily
held.
What is not yet manifest is easily
planned for.
What is still thin is easily broken.
What is still small is easily
scattered.
Deal with things before they
come into fruition.
Set things in order before there is
disorder.

A tree too wide to wrap your
arms around grows from a tiny
seed.
A nine-story tower begins with a
single bucket of clay.
A journey of hundreds of miles
begins with lifting a foot.

He who acts ruins.
He who clings loses hold.
Therefore, the sage does not act and thus
does not ruin,
does not cling and thus does not lose
anything.
People pursuing enterprises always fail
in this just before completion.
That's why it is said:
    Careful to the end as you are at
    the beginning,
    and your enterprise will not fail.

So, the sage only desires freedom from
desires,
and does not covet things just because
they are hard to obtain.
Learning the art of unlearning, he returns
to what the people missed.
But to help the world return to what is *of
itself* so—
he cannot presume to act upon it.

Comments

☯ This verse must rival verse 1 for the most famous line in the Tao Te Ching. Ironically, it might claim its fame somewhat anonymously. Who has not heard or quoted a version of the classic "journey of a thousand miles" line, yet how many know it is from the Tao Te Ching?

☯ Over the years, and especially recently, I've become more and more convinced that this verse may have as much (or more) to do with preventing trouble while it is manageable, as with its frequent *big things come to those who get started* (or similar) interpretation. Look at Mabry's "Correct problems before they occur. Intervene before chaos erupts." Look at Martin 2's "All trouble begins in the mind," or Beaulac's "A tree [problem?] too wide to wrap your arms around grows from a tiny seed." This is not to discount the more standard interpretation at all, but it is to suggest that especially when paired with verse 63, this verse has another message as well. And it is a message worth noting.

☯ Ellen Chen (1989, 200) echoes similar thoughts: "[Verses 63–65] are on . . . the small or incipient state of things . . . when they are pliant and full of rejuvenating power. Once events become full grown they are intractable."

65
Non-knowing

Beaulac

It's said that the ancient ones, skilled
  in the practice of the Way,
did not enlighten the people with
  knowledge,
but made sure they could remain
  simple.
What makes the people unruly is
  knowledge.
    Thus, ruling by knowledge brings
      ruin to a country;
    Ruling by not-knowing brings
      Virtue to a country.
Who understands these two
  principles knows the normative
  model.
This is called deep virtue!
Deep virtue reaches deep and reaches
  far
to gather all things to return,
and therein they realize the Great
  Harmony.

65
Non-knowing

Mabry

In ancient times those who followed
  the Tao
Did not try to educate the people.
They chose to let them be.

The reason people become hard to
  govern
Is that they think they know it all.
So, if a leader tries to lead through
  cleverness,
He is nothing but a liability.
But if a leader leads, not through
  cleverness,
but through goodness, this is a
  blessing to all.

To be always conscious of the Great
  Pattern
is a spiritual virtue.

Spiritual virtue is awesome and
  infinite
And it leads all things back to their
  Source.
Then there emerges the Great
  Harmony.

Non-knowing

Mitchell

The ancient Masters
didn't try to educate the people,
but kindly taught them to not-know.

When they think that they know the
    answers,
people are difficult to guide.
When they know that they don't
    know,
people can find their own way.

If you want to learn how to govern,
avoid being clever or rich.
The simplest pattern is the clearest.
Content with an ordinary life,
you can show all people the way
back to their own true nature.

Comments

☻ An ancient parable, often told in the martial arts, in one of its many variations, recounts the tale of the Master and the visiting scholar, who requested an audience to seek help and advice. The scholar, however, kept countering the Master's teachings with his own opinions. The Master suggested taking tea and when pouring for the visitor, let his pouring overflow until the visitor said, "Stop! Can't you see the cup is too full for more?!" "Exactly," said the Master kindly, "come back when your cup is empty." The scholar sat, then smiled, then understood and went away wiser.

☻ It seems clear, especially looking at Mitchell's or Mabry's 2nd stanza, that this idea of the "empty cup" (also known as *Beginner's Mind* the *Socratic paradox,* or even *the Don't-Know-Mind*) is the direction this verse is pointing, especially as it refers to wise governing that allows/encourages simplicity.

☻ To the extent that the verse applies to our own growth, it nicely echoes the thoughts of verse 48 (Mastery).

☻ What Beaulac calls *deep virtue* is one of those Tao Te Ching phrases which is rendered in several ways. See Further Comments for some of them.

Humility

Breed

The reason the great rivers and the
sea
receive tribute from the valley
streams
is that the rivers and the sea lie lower
than the valleys,
and thus their humility gives them
power.
So it is with the wise person.
If you wish to be lifted up above
others,
humble yourself below them.
If you wish to lead them,
be willing to walk behind them.
In this way, even though you are
above others,
they will not be burdened by your
weight.
Though you lead them, they are not
injured.
People will naturally and effortlessly
lift you up.
If you do not strive against people,
no one will strive against you.

Humility

Mair 29

The river and sea can be kings of
the hundred valley streams
because they are good at
lying below them.
For this reason,
They can be kings of the hundred
valley streams.
For this reason, too,
If the sage wants to be above the
people,
in his words, he must put
himself below them;
If he wishes to be before the
people,
in his person, he must stand
behind them.
Therefore,
He is situated in front of the
people,
but they are not offended;
He is situated above the people,
but they do not consider him a
burden.
All under heaven happily push
him forward without wearying.
Is this not because he is without
contention?
Therefore,
No one under heaven can contend
with him.

66
Humility

Hogan

An ocean is greater than the hundred
    rivers that flow into it,
and all it does is wait to receive what
    they bring.

If you want to teach people, don't
    talk down to them.
If you want to lead them, find out
    where they want to go.

People love leaders who make them
    feel safe
without smothering them.
They'll always support a leader like
    that,
and because he doesn't try to
    compete with anybody,
nobody is able to compete with him.

Comments

☯ Another return to the theme of the sea/ocean and the tributaries that flow into them. The verse continues to point to the themes of Humility, greater/lesser, and higher/lower, as well as good rulers and leaders and, in so doing, echoes the thoughts in verse 61 (Yielding) and other similar verses.

☯ And while the mild puzzlement expressed in comment 61 continues for me, I'm always helped a little in *this* verse by a couple of the particular translations and comments.

☯ Mair's translation, included here, for example, seems to help with some overall perspective, regardless of its wordy nature. And a line from Mitchell's comments is also helpful. Referring to the master being "above the people," he writes, "Not that she feels superior, but that, looking from a higher vantage point, she can see more."

☯ I'm reminded that it is also true that the ocean perpetuates its existence *because of* the tributaries, and yet they all flow toward—as in look to—the ocean. It seems that neither exists without the other and each honors the other. And yet the ocean is still somehow *greater*.

Treasures

Breed

All the world says that while my Tao
is great,
it yet appears to be inferior to other
systems of teaching.
Its very greatness is what makes it
seem to be inferior.
If it were like any other system,
then its true smallness would have
been revealed by now!
But I have three precious things I
value and hold fast.
The first is gentleness, the second is
simplicity,
and the third is humility.
With gentleness I can be bold;
with simplicity I can be generous;
shrinking from taking precedence
over others,
I am married to honor.
Nowadays people give up gentleness
and are all for being bold;
they give up simplicity, and are all
for being liberal;
they aren't willing to be humble
and seek only to be foremost.
All this ends in death.
Gentleness is sure to be victorious
even in battle.
It firmly maintains its ground.
If you are kind and gentle,
Heaven will save you.
Your very gentleness will protect
you.

67

Treasures

Bynner

Everyone says that my way of life is
the way of a simpleton.
Being largely the way of a simpleton
is what makes it worth while.
If it were not the way of a simpleton
It would long ago have been
worthless,
These possessions of a simpleton
being the three I choose
And cherish:
To care,
To be fair,
To be humble.
When a man cares he is unafraid,
When he is fair he leaves enough for
others,
When he is humble he can grow;
Whereas if, like men of today, he be
bold without caring,
Self-indulgent without sharing,
Self-important without shame,
He is dead.
The invincible shield
Of caring
Is a weapon from the sky
Against being dead.

67
Treasures

Martin

No one sees anything special about
    this path.
Yet it is because it appears ordinary
that it remains wondrous.
No one has been able to market it.
No one has trivialized it.

There are three virtues inherent in
    this path:
compassion, simplicity, and patience.
Wherever there is compassion,
fear does not abide.
Wherever there is simplicity,
generosity resides.
Wherever there is patience,
all things are accomplished.

If we try to be fearless
and do not have compassion,
we become ruthless.
If we try to be generous
and do not have simplicity,
we become controlling.
If we try to accomplish things
and do not have patience,
we become failures.

Compassion is the root of all these
    virtues.
It is the very nature of the Tao.
It is the energy that binds all things
    together.

Comments

☺ The *three treasures* verse, in which Lao Tzu shares the three treasures (or virtues) he values most (and teaches) in his life. He goes on to relate these to each other, expounding on the subtle dangers of having one or two without the other(s).

☺ Even more than usual, it seems, there are so many choices for the wordings surrounding these three treasures (*many* of which can be seen in Further Comments), but they all seem to eventually settle on some variation of compassion (gentleness, caring) as the one that is above the others.

☺ The three treasures of this verse, along with these corresponding indicators pointing to the greatest of them, present a striking similarity to I Corinthians 13:13 (NIV): "And now these three remain: faith, hope and love. But the greatest of these is love."

68
Non-aggression

Feng & English

A good soldier is not violent.
A good fighter is not angry.
A good winner is not vengeful.
A good employer is humble.
This is known as the Virtue of not
striving.
This is known as ability to deal with
people.
This since ancient times has been
known as the ultimate unity with
heaven.

68
Non-aggression

Breed

The person who follows the Tao does
not use force.
She does not lose her temper.
She does not engage with her foes.
When she leads, she does so with
humility.
We look at her and say,
"She never contends with others.
That is what makes her strong.
She persuades others
to use their own strength for
harmony.
She lives in harmony with Heaven's
light."

68
Non-aggression

Martin

When confrontation arises
we face it without aggression.
When someone opposes us
we do not give in to anger.
We view no one as a competitor
because we do not seek our own way.

We know our strengths
and we know our weaknesses.
We use them each for benefit.
We are not trying to fix ourselves or
    others
so we move naturally and easily
    along our path.

Comments

☯ Ellen Chen makes comments for both verses 68 and 69 that seem to shed light on both verses. She says that this verse (68) "applies the three treasures of the preceding chapter to the condition of both peace and war" (Chen 1989, 211).

☯ The point here and in most translations seems to be that in all things, from minor confrontation to the waging of war, the spirit of Non-aggression should be at work. One does not *seek* war—or even conflict—and fights (or quarrels?) with sorrow when it is unavoidable. This certainly seems in harmony with the sentiments of verse 67.

☯ See Further Comments for other translations (besides those here) of Feng & English's "Virtue of not striving."

69

Enemies

Mitchell

The generals have a saying:
"Rather than make the first move
it is better to wait and see.
Rather than advance an inch
it is better to retreat a yard."

This is called
going forward without advancing,
pushing back without using
    weapons.

There is no greater misfortune
than underestimating your enemy.
Underestimating your enemy
means thinking that he is evil.
Thus you destroy your three
    treasures
and become an enemy yourself.

When two great forces oppose each
    other,
the victory will go
to the one that knows how to yield.

69

Enemies

Martin

Military strategists agree.
They would rather defend
than make a foolish attack.
They would rather consolidate
than overextend.

So we move forward
without conquering anyone.
We gain
without anyone losing.
We confront obstacles
without using weapons.

We call no one enemy,
for to call someone enemy
is to lose our inner unity.
We become divided against ourselves
and everyone suffers.

When conflict arises
we refuse to separate ourselves.
This is how we remain at peace.

69
Enemies

Mabry

The military has a saying:

> "I would rather be passive, like a
>   guest
> than aggressive, like a host.
> I would rather retreat a foot
> than advance an inch."

> This is called going forward
>   without instigating,
> Engaging without force
> Defense without hatred
> Victory without weapons.

There is no greater calamity than
  underestimating the enemy.
If I take my enemy too lightly, I am
  in danger of losing my
compassion, moderation, and
  non-competitive spirit.

So, when two armies confront each
  other
Victory will go to them that grieve.

Comments

☯ Ellen Chen continues her thoughts on connecting verses 68 and 69 to 67 by noting that this is "how a Taoist ruler fights, or rather avoids, a war" (Chen 1989, 212), which seems to succinctly sum up the theme of this verse.

☯ The references back to verse 67 are more pronounced in this verse, as one sees Mabry's "I am in danger of losing my compassion, moderation, and non-competitive spirit" and in Mitchell's "underestimating your enemy . . . you destroy your three treasures."

70
Understanding

Mabry

My words are very easy to
    understand
And very easy to practice.
Yet the World is not able to
    understand
Nor able to put them into practice.

My words speak of the primal.
My deeds are but service.
Unless people understand this
They won't understand me.
And since so few understand me,
Then such understanding is rare and
    valuable indeed.

Therefore the Sage wears common
    clothes
And hides his treasures only in his
    heart.

70
Understanding

Martin

Our conditioned ways
of seeing things and doing things
make it hard for us to understand.
But this path is easy to find
and easy to follow.

This path arises from the source of
    all.
Its power enlivens all things.
If we learn to know this source,
we learn to know ourselves.

Following this path we are led
to the inner treasure of our being.
Our outer trappings remain simple
so we are free to cherish our inner
    joy.

70
Understanding

Bynner

My way is so simple to feel, so easy
    to apply,
That only a few will feel it or apply
    it.
If it were not the lasting way, the
    natural way to try,
If it were a passing way, everyone
    would try it.
But however few shall go my way
Or feel concerned with me,
Some there are and those are they
Who witness what they see:
Sanity is a haircloth sheath
With a jewel underneath.

Comments

☯ "And if he didn't laugh, it wouldn't be Tao" (verse 41). If we're honest, I suspect we all have a little trouble getting past the first couple of lines of a traditional rendition of this verse. "Easy to understand"? "Easy to put into practice"? Yeah, right, Old Fella! What else are you trying to sell? And yet . . . And *yet* . . .

☯ And yet, have we not all noticed at some point how easily and perfectly Mother Nature's world follows this path, this Way? Animals. Birds in the air. Fish in the sea. Even trees, plants, and "the lilies of the field" (Matthew 6:28). Are there any better disciples? So . . . what/where is the difference? Is it our unique phenomenon of human *intellect* (and/or *consciousness*) that makes practicing the Tao (participating in the Way) difficult?

☯ Yes and no, perhaps. I think Martin's translation here begins to help. Our intellect is our greatest gift. It is what makes us *human*, with all that entails and allows. It is a marvelous servant, but a horrible master. It is our intellect that leads to our ability to create our individual and cultural conditioning, which in turn can keep us distracted from "the inner treasure of our being" (!). The intellect tries to *lead* our lives instead of *live* them (as nature does). No wonder it can't grasp Lao Tzu's words or allow us to practice them.

71
Mind

Beaulac

Knowing you don't know is best;
not knowing you don't know brings
   affliction.
The sage is without affliction
   because,
recognizing afflictions for what they
   are,
she stays free from them.

71
Mind

Martin 2

Pretending to know the mysteries of
   existence
is true folly.
Not knowing the suffering caused by
   our own mind,
is ignorance indeed.
When we know the origins of
   suffering found within ourselves,
then we actually know something.
Then we are truly free.

71
Mind

Mair 36

To realize that you do not
    understand is a virtue;
Not to realize that you do not
    understand is a defect.

The reason why
    The sage has no defects,
    Is because he treats defects as
        defects.

Thus,
    He has no defects.

Comments

☯ And, speaking of the intellect (verse 70), this verse continues that theme while stirring in a large dose of verse 65 (Non-knowing) as well. And what a fascinating result!

☯ I'm continually re-attracted to Martin's phrasing, "Not knowing the suffering caused by our own mind, is ignorance indeed." How often have we heard the phrase, "It's all in your mind"? More and more lately, influenced by Tao verses like this one, I've become increasingly tempted to ask, "What if this is *literally* true?!" What if it's *all* in your mind?! Is that what Mair's 2nd stanza is trying to say, that the sage realizes the "defects" are in his mind and his thinking, and "Thus, he has no defects"?

☯ So yes, I think verses 70 and 71 are saying, almost in unison, "get your mind out of it (humbly and willingly), and things won't seem so puzzling." (As if that's easy!)

☯ Looking back now at the mind's role in the *leading*-a-life-versus-*living*-a-life thought in the previous verses, I'm somehow reminded of Washington's remark in the musical *Hamilton* (and I can hear the cadence!), "Dying is easy young man, living is harder."

Awe

Mitchell

When they lose their sense of awe,
people turn to religion.
When they no longer trust
    themselves,
they begin to depend upon authority.

Therefore the Master steps back
so that people won't be confused.
He teaches without a teaching,
so that people will have nothing to
    learn.

Awe

Martin

If we have no awe of mystery,
we are easily controlled by fear.
We constrict ourselves with self-hate
and become willing victims of other
    people.

Knowing our true nature,
we see ourselves clearly,
but do not become arrogant.
We cherish ourselves,
but not as separate from all other
    beings.
Our external identity
is nourished by our inner reality.

72
Awe

Feng & English

When men lack a sense of awe, there
  will be disaster.

Do not intrude in their homes.
Do not harass them at work.
If you do not interfere, they will not
  weary of you.

Therefore, the sage knows himself
  but makes no show,
Has self-respect but is not arrogant.
He lets go of that and chooses this.

Comments

☯ *One* of the reasons for the three choices for this verse is that all three of them open with some sort of reference to the Awe of the Tao and its inherently divine mysteries. It turns out that this inclusion is the exception rather than the rule in this verse, as most authors omit such direct reference.

☯ This omission may be for a variety of translation reasons, of course. But, one of my personal treasures, over the years of reading the Tao Te Ching, is the realization of a gradual awakening of a delightful and hard-to-describe sense of Awe, especially in the little things that are hiding in plain sight every day. (See also verses 14 and 25.)

☯ In each of the three translations here, there are also subtle warnings connected to the loss of Awe in our lives. Particularly striking is Martin's connecting of lack of Awe with increase of fear. Isn't it interesting to note fear's ever-so-subtle and nebulous influence over the decisions we make?

☯ And in reading Mitchell's last stanza, I also hear—for the second straight verse—strong echoes of verse 65 (Non-knowing).

Net

Beaulac

The courage to take bold actions
    often gets one killed;
the courage to not take bold actions
    preserves life.
But for either of these, there is
    sometimes benefit, sometimes
    harm.
Who knows why heaven rejects what
    it does?
Heaven's Way
    does not fight, yet is excellent at
      winning;
    does not speak, yet has perfect
      response;
    is not summoned, yet appears on
      its own;
    is never hurried nor worried, yet
      plans excellently.
Heaven's net is vast, and though
    wide-meshed, nothing slips past it.

73
Net

Martin 2

We can only do the best we know to
    do.
We cannot predict the outcomes of
    our actions.
We may do harm when we meant
    only good;
and the harm we do may end up for
    the good.
Who knows?
Not even the Sage.
But if we remain centered and calm
regardless of circumstances,
we will be able to respond
with presence, patience,
and helpful action.
We don't know what will happen
as we travel along this path,
but we will never lose our way.

73
Net

Feng & English

A brave and passionate man will kill
    or be killed.
A brave and calm man will always
    preserve life.
Of these two which is good and
    which is harmful?
Some things are not favored by
    heaven. Who knows why?
Even the sage is unsure of this.

The Tao of heaven does not strive,
    and yet it overcomes.
It does not speak, and yet is
    answered.
It does not ask, yet is supplied with
    all its needs.
It seems to have no aim and yet its
    purpose is fulfilled.

Heaven's net casts wide.
Though its meshes are coarse,
    nothing slips through.

Comments

☯ Ah, another age-old question here: "How do I know if my actions will help or hurt in the long run?" This verse gives a surprisingly short and to-the-point answer—you don't. Not even the sage knows.

☯ At the same time, the general vibes from the verse seem to remove some of the drama from the question, even if not in so many words. Martin 2's beautiful last line assures us that, centered in the Tao, we won't lose our way, and most other translations refer to nothing slipping through heaven's Net, which I take to mean that nothing is missed (by heaven) in the grand scheme of things.

☯ These thoughts, especially with Martin 2's phrasing, could perhaps be viewed as the Tao Te Ching's version of the sentiments in Romans 8:28 (KJV), "All things work together for good to them that love God."

74
Control

Mitchell

If you realize that all things change,
there is nothing you will try to hold
    on to.
If you aren't afraid of dying,
there is nothing you can't achieve.

Trying to control the future
is like trying to take the master
    carpenter's place.
When you handle the master
    carpenter's tools,
chances are that you'll cut yourself.

74
Control

Beaulac

If people do not fear death, why
    threaten them with capital
    punishment?
If they are under constant dread of
    death, yet still act unlawfully,
then those we catch and arrest we'd
    have to kill,
and who would dare do that?
There is already a Grim Reaper, and
    taking his place is like
stepping in to wield the blade of a
    master wood-carver.
Whoever does this rarely escapes
    injuring himself.

74
Control

Bynner

Death is no threat to people
Who are not afraid to die;
But even if these offenders feared
    death all day,
Who should be rash enough
To act as executioner?
Nature is executioner.
When man usurps the place,
A carpenter's apprentice takes the
    place of the master:
And 'an apprentice hacking with the
    master's axe
May slice his own hand.'

Comments

☯ In most translations, depending on the variation of focus, this verse is an indictment of capital punishment, excessive punishment, tyranny of government, and/or even killing in general. And most translations contain some kind of hint that power over life and death rests in the hands of heaven, with a hard-to-forget image, in that context, of the damage done from an apprentice using the master's tools.

☯ Both Mitchell (included here) and Martin move away from that focus to the slightly broader issues of the futility of trying to Control one's environment, with Martin mixing in an unnatural fear of death.

☯ In some sense, this verse also continues verse 73's theme of uncertainty related to an action's outcomes. Mitchell (see Further Comments) even includes in his notes a classic old Good/Bad-Who's-to-Say? parable which, were it not related to his focus on Control in this verse, almost seems more suited to the theme of verse 73.

75

Empowering

Mabry

The people are starving because their
     leaders
eat up all their money in taxes.
And so, they are hungry.

The people are rebellious
because their leaders are intrusive.
And so, they protest.

The people make light of death
     because their leaders
live so well at their expense.
And so, they expect death.

Therefore, it seems that one who
     does not grasp this life
too tightly is better off than one who
     clings.

75

Empowering

Beaulac

The reason people are starving
is because their rulers eat up too
     much tax-grain.
That's why they starve.
The reason the people are
     difficult to govern
is because their rulers always find
     reasons for meddlesome
     actions.
That's why they become difficult
     to govern.
The reason the people are
     unconcerned about death
is because having to strive for life
     has made it burdensome.
That's why they're unconcerned
     about death.

Truly, one who does not strive for
     life is even wiser than one who
     reveres life.

75
Empowering

Legge

The people suffer from famine because of the multitude of taxes consumed by their superiors. It is through this that they suffer famine.

The people are difficult to govern because of the (excessive) agency of their superiors (in governing them). It is through this that they are difficult to govern.

The people make light of dying because of the greatness of their labours in seeking for the means of living. It is this which makes them think light of dying. Thus it is that to leave the subject of living altogether out of view is better than to set a high value on it.

Comments

❂ The first stanza(s) here seem(s) to pick right up from verse 74 as the focus on tyrannical governing becomes a much stronger indictment.

❂ But the verse is also like verse 74 in its apparent focus on death, especially as the people's anger and rebelliousness toward their leaders' actions turns to resignation and defeat. Beaulac indicates that their "having to strive for life" makes them "unconcerned about death."

❂ Mair (40.10, 111), however, has a most interesting point which may cast light on the last part of this verse. He points out that "many ancient Chinese leaders were almost fanatical in their pursuit of longevity," and he even lists some of their "bizarre regimens and extravagant practices." It seems likely Lao Tzu might be aiming some of his final (otherwise obscure?) words at these leaders and practices. Indeed, as you read Mabry's rendition of the last line, can you not feel Lao Tzu's sentiment aimed in that direction rather pointedly?

Flexible

Beaulac

When life begins we are supple and
  tender.
When life ends we are rigid and
  unyielding.
All things, including the grass and
  trees,
are pliant and supple in life,
and dry and rigid in death.
So the supple and tender are
  companions of life,
While the stiff and unyielding are
  companions of death.
> An army that cannot yield is
>   defeated.
> A tree that can't bend cracks in
>   the wind.
> The strong and great are laid low
> while the soft and gentle prevail.

Flexible

Martin

Before we are conditioned
by all the "dos and don'ts" of life,
we are naturally tender and gentle.
As we grow old,
we constrict around these conditions
and end up dying stiff and rigid.
Indeed all living things begin soft
    and supple
and end up brittle and dry.

So we see that hardness and
    inflexibility
are signs of death,
and that tenderness and gentleness
are signs of life.

It is the ability of an army to change
    its plans
that keeps it from defeat.
It is the ability of a tree to bend in the
    wind
that keeps it from toppling.
Our natural tenderness
is our true strength.

76
Flexible

Mair 41

Human beings are
    soft and supple when alive,
    stiff and straight when dead.

The myriad creatures, the grasses
  and trees are
    soft and fragile when alive,
    dry and withered when dead.

Therefore, it is said:
  The rigid person is a disciple of
    death;
  The soft, supple, and delicate are
    lovers of life.

An army that is inflexible will not
  conquer;
A tree that is inflexible will snap.

The unyielding and mighty shall
  be brought low;
The soft, supple, and delicate will
  be set above.

Comments

☯ I've heard it said that as people age, they tend to go one of two opposite directions—they either grow crabbier and more inflexible, or they become softer and easier to deal with. Whether that's true in general or not, this verse seems to provide a prescription for assuring we can achieve the latter. Stay Flexible, yield to events we can't control—indeed, go with the flow.

☯ Flexibility, yielding, softness. Most translations remind us we start that way physically when we are young. Martin goes a step further and reminds us these qualities are actually part of our true inner nature. I like that perspective and that reminder.

☯ But these Taoist qualities are often considered weak in today's mile-a-minute, gotta-get-ahead society. This verse—especially in its last lines—underscores their importance in our daily lives and the inherent danger of ignoring their cultivation. As Martin says, "Our natural tenderness is our true strength."

77

Balance

Beaulac

The Way of Heaven is like the
 drawing of a bow:
    The higher part is drawn
      downward,
    and the lower part draws upward.
    Where there is excess it
      diminishes;
    and where there is lack, it
      supplies.

Heaven's Way takes from what is
 excessive, and supplements what
 isn't enough.
Humanity's way is not like this, is it?
We take from those not having
 enough and make offerings to the
 rich.
Who can find the abundance and give
 it to the world? Only a person of
 the Way.
And so the sage:
    acts without claiming merit,
    accomplishes without dwelling
    on it.
In being like this, there is no desire to
 be seen as virtuous.

77

Balance

Martin

Following this path is like stringing a
 bow.
One end is pulled down
and the other is pulled up,
creating a dynamic balance.
So this practice encourages a
 dynamic balance
between excess and deficiency.
When we see an excess,
we reduce it.
When we see a deficiency,
we give to it.

This is contrary to common wisdom.
Common wisdom seeks
to constantly increase excess.
To do this, that which is lacking
must decrease even more.
Balance is destroyed.

To keep balance we must trust this
 path
and keep to our true nature.
This allows us to give without worry,
and to receive without attachment.

Balance

Legge

May not the Way (or Tao) of Heaven be compared to the (method of) bending a bow? The (part of the bow) which was high is brought low, and what was low is raised up. (So Heaven) diminishes where there is superabundance, and supplements where there is deficiency.

It is the Way of Heaven to diminish superabundance, and to supplement deficiency. It is not so with the way of man. He takes away from those who have not enough to add to his own superabundance.

Who can take his own superabundance and therewith serve all under heaven? Only he who is in possession of the Tao!

Therefore the (ruling) sage acts without claiming the results as his; he achieves his merit and does not rest (arrogantly) in it:—he does not wish to display his superiority.

Comments

☯ In the same way verse 76 focuses on our need to stay flexible, this verse picks up the theme and reminds us of the importance of Balance as well. These two qualities are not quite the same, of course, but they go hand in hand, as being flexible can certainly lead to better Balance, both physically and emotionally.

☯ This particular kind of Balance, as described in the first half of the verse, is special and plays an important role in our lives, and also in our dealings with others. It allows us, as Martin says, "to give without worry and receive without attachment," and as Beaulac says, "[act] without claiming credit, [accomplish] without dwelling on it." I'm not sure I ever thought about the fact that selfless acts like that *do* indeed require a unique (and difficult) kind of *Balance*. And portraying Balance with those images helps remind us that Balance is— besides being harder than it looks—a worthy goal to pursue.

78
Paradoxical

Beaulac

Below Heaven there is nothing so
  soft and yielding as water.
And yet for attacking the strong and
  unyielding, nothing surpasses it.
For this reason, nothing can take its
  place.
    The yielding overcomes the
      unyielding,
    and the soft overcomes the hard.
Everyone recognizes this, but few
  practice it.
Therefore the sage says:
    Who takes the country's
      dishonors on oneself
    is worthy of the sacred offerings
      for soil and grain;
    Who takes a country's
      misfortunes on oneself
    is worthy of being king.
(Straight truth often sounds twisted.)

78
Paradoxical

Martin

This path seems paradoxical.
Like water, it is soft and yielding,
yet there is no better way to
    overcome
the stiffness and rigidity
that causes so much suffering.

We intuitively know that flexibility
is more effective than stubbornness
and that tenderness is superior
to hard-heartedness,
yet our conditioned habits keep us
from acting on this knowledge.

By accepting all that seems humble
    and plain,
we become masters of every
    situation.
By opening our hearts
to all that seems painful and difficult,
we help end all suffering.
No wonder it seems paradoxical.

78
Paradoxical

Hogan

Nothing is softer or more yielding
than water.
Yet, given time, it can erode even the
hardest stone.
That's how the weak can defeat the
strong,
and the supple can win out over the
stiff.

Everybody knows it.
So why don't we apply it to our own
lives?

Lao Tzu used to say:
"Take on people's problems, and you
can be their leader.
Deal with the world's problems, and
you'll be a Master."

Sometimes the truth makes no sense.

Comments

☯ Lao Tzu breaks out one of his favorite topics—the nature and power of water—to seemingly revisit verse 76 and remind us of the importance of softness, yielding, and flexibility as the way to help us lead an effective life.

☯ Yet, at the same time, he wisely acknowledges the problem. On the one hand, he wonders (as perhaps do we?) why it seems so hard to apply water's example to our own lives. And on the other, he acknowledges how paradoxical it all sounds. (Look at the last lines of each translation here.)

☯ A one-word comment I found buried in my notes has at least helped me with this dilemma lately. Next to lines about yielding always overcoming, I had written "slowly." Sure, the *power* of (the softness and flexibility of) water can conquer the biggest obstacles—look at the Grand Canyon. But it won't happen overnight—look at the Grand Canyon.

☯ Thinking we can adopt flexibility as a short-term strategy to win something may not be effective. It likely needs to be an ongoing adoption, and probably involves considerable patience as well.

Integrity

Legge

When a reconciliation is effected
(between two parties) after a great
animosity, there is sure to be a
grudge remaining (in the mind of the
one who was wrong). And how can
this be beneficial (to the other)?

Therefore (to guard against this), the
sage keeps the left-hand portion of
the record of the engagement, and
does not insist on the (speedy)
fulfilment of it by the other party.
(So), he who has the attributes (of the
Tao) regards (only) the conditions of
the engagement, while he who has
not those attributes regards only the
conditions favourable to himself.

In the Way of Heaven, there is no
partiality of love; it is always on the
side of the good man.

79

Integrity

Martin 2

Seeking advantage over others is not
    the way of Tao.
Blaming others will not solve
    problems.
Be content with your own work and
    correct your own mistakes.
Seek ways to give
instead of ways to get.
The Tao has no favorites
but you will be happiest
when you align yourself with its
    flow.

Integrity

Mair 44

Compromise with great
    resentment
        will surely yield lingering
        resentment;
How can this be seen as good?

For this reason,
    The sage holds the debtor's side
        of a contract
            and does not make claims
            upon others.

Therefore,
    The man of integrity attends to
        his debts;
    The man without integrity attends
        to his exactions.

The Way of heaven is impartial,
    yet is always with the good
        person.

Comments

☯ Even before paper, the ancient Chinese kept track of debts by putting the agreement on bamboo (or similar) and then splitting it lengthwise to form an interlocking record of the debt. The left, or *inferior,* side went to the borrower and the right to the lender, who could demand payment at any time by presenting his side.

☯ This verse is suggesting that to avoid resentments in any debts or even disagreements (and probably in general as well), the sage, or man of Integrity, should behave as if he held the debtor's portion and "not make claims upon others" (Mair).

☯ Even Martin 2, who avoids the historical debtor/lender terminology, suggests that we "seek ways to give instead of ways to get." Anything else, it seems, can not only lead to resentment, but to distraction from the impartiality of the Way, as well.

Ideal

Beaulac

Societies should be no larger than
villages.
Then there is no need for an
abundance of inventions.
People who understand mortality
stop running to and fro;
even with an abundance of
transports, there is no need for them.
And if they have armaments, there is
no occasion to display them.
Let life be simple enough for:
    remembering things by knotting a
    string,
    making good meals and beautiful
    clothing,
    enjoying the peacefulness of
    home,
    and finding joy in the everyday.

Villages close enough to hear each
other's dogs and roosters,
could live their entire lives without
feeling compelled to travel back and
forth.

Martin 2

A society should be arranged as a
    small village,
content with the simple life.
Technology may offer wonders
    without number,
but they are seldom used.
Vehicles may move with amazing
    speed,
but they remain idle.
Weapons may be sophisticated and
    deadly,
but they remain locked away
    gathering dust.

The moment to moment enjoyment
    of food and family,
gardens and community,
work and leisure,
bring contentment and joy to life.
One who lives this way
will come to old age and death
with the complete satisfaction
of a fully lived life.

80
Ideal

Hogan

Lao Tzu had a dream about a small
  country with very few people.

They didn't need machines to get
  their work done faster.
They took their lives seriously, and
  stayed closed to home.

They may have owned boats and
  carriages,
but they never went anywhere.
They may have owned weapons,
but they kept those weapons locked
  up, securely hidden.
They had so few responsibilities,
they never had to make a To-Do list
  to remember what had to be
  done.

They enjoyed simple foods,
dressed plainly, lived comfortably,
and kept their traditions alive.

And even though their neighbors
  were so close
they could hear the dogs barking at
  night,
they had no interest in leaving their
  homes,
where they grew old peacefully and
  died.

Comments

☯ What an idyllic scene this verse
paints! Each time I read it, in spite of
myself, I feel like I'm in the middle of a
Norman Rockwell painting. It can feel
very peaceful.

☯ I say "in spite of myself," because I
think there are a couple of conclusions
we should *not* leap to here in terms of
the verse's message.

☯ The first is that, as previously
mentioned, I do not believe that this
verse (or the Tao Te Ching, in general)
should be interpreted as anti-travel. See
verse 47 and the comments there.

☯ Nor do I believe that the verse (or the
Tao Te Ching, in general) should be
interpreted as anti-progress. I believe the
Tao Te Ching's core messages apply to
the world of today, including all its
changes and gadgets, with no less
pertinence than the 500 BCE world of
Lao Tzu's ancient China. I'm reminded
of Feng & English's verse 14 excerpt
(see comment there): "Stay with the
ancient Tao, / Move with the present."

☯ Instead I believe the main message
here is one of contentment and
simplicity, as is consistent with the same
message in earlier verses. Today's world
is certainly different—and certainly
more accessible. Adventure—and
progress—await us as, when, and if we
choose them. But neither the adventure
nor the advances will *replace* anything
that isn't already in us. Regardless of our
environment and opportunities, it is
suggested that we stay content with
ourselves and centered in our simplicity
and authenticity.

81
Nourishing

Mabry

True words are not beautiful.
Beautiful words are not true.

Good people do not argue.
Argumentative people are not good.

The wise are not necessarily
    well-educated.
The well-educated are not necessarily
    wise.

The Sage does not hoard things.
The more she does for others
The more she finds she has.
The more she gives to others
The more she finds she gains.

Heaven's Way is to nourish, not to
    harm.
The Sage's Way is to work, yet not
    compete.

81
Nourishing

Martin 2

The use of eloquent words
will not illuminate this path.
Sophisticated argument
will not convince others of its truth.
Books without number
will not teach this path.
Simplicity is the practical and joyful
    guide
that teaches us this way to walk.
By giving, we receive.
By serving, we gain.
The Tao flows and moves us
as if we were floating with the wind.

81
Nourishing

Breed

Sincerity doesn't worry about being
pleasant.
Pleasant words aren't necessarily
sincere.
Those who follow the Tao most
closely
don't get in arguments about the Tao.
People who love to argue aren't
familiar with the Tao.
Those who know the Tao don't flaunt
their knowledge.
Those who need everyone to
recognize their wisdom
don't know the Tao.
The wise person doesn't accumulate
things for herself.
The more she helps others,
the richer she becomes;
and the more she gives to others,
the more she possesses.
Heaven's way is keen-edged,
but it never injures.
The wise person accomplishes much,
but he never strives.

Comments

☻ After his 81-verse performance, the curtain drops, the house lights come back up, the audience heads for the exits, and Lao Tzu (not unlike Elvis) "has left the building." What a performance! I don't know about you, but I've already got tickets for the next time through, where the show will be identically the same, and yet so very different.

☻ But as he leaves, Lao Tzu's last verse/act reminds us that he had no choice but to do the whole thing with *words*, and that is no small impediment. He has been doing nothing but *pointing*, and he reminds us not to fixate on the finger. Can't you feel him urging us (again, with words!) to follow the direction of the pointing and *discover* the treasure ourselves? Don't be satisfied with listening to the sage, he seems to imply—become the sage! (Note: *No one,* least of all *me*, says this is easy!) And then smile along with him/her. You can still come back for the next performance(s), but you'll have a lifetime pass and a front row center seat!

☻ Go in peace, friend. See you next time through.

Acknowledgments

This book's journey from conception to manifestation has been a winding and scenic one, well off the main interstate. Companions and guides have frequently appeared at just the right times, or it would not have been completed. Here are some for whom I'm extremely grateful.

Bill Martin, author and sage: Bill was first an author whose work spoke to me, then became a correspondence acquaintance, and now I don't think he'd object if I label him as a friend. His books and his communications have been invaluable to my Tao journeys over the past decade, at least. More recently, his gracious carte blanche permission to quote from his *Walking the Tao* book was a most timely godsend in many ways, and his agreement to write the foreword for this book was both generous and an honor. I am lucky to have crossed paths with him, and you will enjoy his translations.

John Mabry, author/publisher at Apocryphile: John was the first publisher to seriously confirm that this book was a viable idea worth pursuing. (He even suggested the title I ended up using!) We have corresponded several times since those formative days, and I'll always appreciate his advice and encouragement, not to mention his helpful fee structure for the use of so many of the verses from the two Apocryphile translations (including his own).

Peter London, Permissions Director at HarperCollins: Peter not only put the lie to "big New York publishers are impersonal, inaccessible, and unfriendly," he single-handedly demolished it, at least for HarperCollins. Peter obviously handles a *huge* number of these permission requests, yet I was consistently *amazed* at his very efficient and professional (and always *so prompt!*) responses, his willingness to help, and the friendly attitude that went with all of that, even through a couple of early non-routine glitches. The phrase "above and beyond" became repetitive, and he began to feel like a long-lost friend, one I might invite to our next Thanksgiving dinner.

Beau Sullivan, Permissions Associate at Penguin Random House: Another genuinely helpful, go-to resource at a large New York publisher. Beau was always cheerful—and patient—through the entire process, and I was glad to get to work with him.

Susie Cook, longtime family friend and fellow explorer of wild ideas: Other than my editor, of course, Susie set the record for most partial drafts read along the way, and all it cost me was an occasional *skinny latte grande* at our local coffee shop! I appreciated her honest and helpful comments and her ongoing encouragement.

Pat; Christi & Josh; and Adam, Licia & Heron—the best family in the known universe: Pat, my rock-solid wife of over a half-century and longest existing companion on the spiritual path. Our individual "Ways" on that journey have each occasionally taken delightfully different and beneficial side paths through the lands of the mystics from time to time, but we've always had the other one in sight, thankfully for me. Christi, our daughter, was lucky enough to inherit her mom's good looks but unlucky enough to inherit her father's weird sense of humor. She always keeps me laughing and always brightens any day that has a phone visit or a text. Adam, our son, has always been there to good-naturedly prod me when my feet get cold on an adventure. This time, he was the first to officially suggest out loud using a comment page instead of a fourth translation. He did this at just the perfect time in the process, and that helped me gradually regain momentum when it had taken an unannounced vacation. How I love this entire crew!

And, finally, Anita Dixon, the project's editor-and-more, and the *sine non qua* of its completion: Anita has survived a few challenges working for and with me at various times and projects over the years, since our professor/student days, and has even edited one of my earlier books, so she's no stranger to tasks that endanger one's metal health. But this latest one may have taken the cake. Besides being an excellent sounding board and suggestion-maker, Anita is also, thank God, an expert at (and a stickler for) anything that involves a style manual and/or *anything* to do with punctuation, grammar and all shapes of rules relating to these occasional arbitrary mysteries. Combine this with proofing skills that can spot a period upside down, and she's worth her weight in gold. The trouble is, she has to work with (and for) someone who, despite his grammar-pride, is not only woefully lacking in some of those more esoteric skills but has his own warped vision of what *some* of those rules *really should* be, and then pulls rank! So I say this without one ounce of hyperbole and with absolute conviction: If you find *anything* even askance (let alone wrong) in this book, I *guarantee* it is a result of an oversight on my part or, worse (and more likely), a deliberate "Let's do it this way!" from me. It's easy to toss around the phrase "I couldn't have done it without her!" but what do you do when that's a rather ineffective understatement?

FURTHER COMMENTS

Continued comments and notes for some verses are listed below. References here are endnotes and are found at the end of the section.

Verse 1

☯ Verse 1 may be the most famous of the Tao Te Ching's verses, and it may also be the one that most completely captures the book's overall message in a nutshell. Red Pine (1996, 3), in his notes on this verse, quotes Te-Ch'ing: "Lao-Tzu's philosophy is all here. The remaining five thousand words only expand on this first verse."

☯ A variety of notes and commentaries for this important introductory verse occur in several different translations. Individually, they take different approaches to what they highlight; collectively they provide a wealth of background and historical material. Here are *some* highlights: Mair (45, 111) focuses on the first four lines. Beaulac gives a broad overview of the whole verse, with translation notes. Chen's comments (1989, 51–55) are most detailed, covering a *wide* range. Needleman (F&E) has a short overview, followed by an insightful look at desire. Mitchell provides a variety of general comments and notes.

☯ I can identify with trying to describe something by having to share what it's *not*. Forgive my *math education* detour, but to begin to enlighten future (especially elementary) teachers—and indeed, sometimes "the man in the street"—about what mathematics really *is*, one has to start with what it's *not (only)*. It's *not (only)*—if even much anymore—times tables, rote memorization, paper/pencil calculations and the like, ad infinitum. One might even say, "The Math that can be calculated by rote is not the Math that solves problems." That has the same advantage as the first line in verse 1: it is an excellent pointer, but is nebulous in its description.

Verse 2

One of the reasons Mitchell's referenced comment about the Tao writing the script appeals to me is that it echoes repeated references from Joseph Campbell about the same thing. In many places, Campbell refers to an essay by Schopenhauer ("On an Apparent Intention in the Fate of the Individual"): He notes that "Schopenhauer points out that when you reach an advanced age, as I have, and look back over your lifetime, it can seem to have had a plot, as though composed by some novelist. Events that when they occurred had seemed accidental or incidental turn out to have been indispensable factors in the composition. So who composed that plot?"[1]

Verse 5

Mair (49.2, 4; 112), Beaulac, and Feng & English (among others) all use the straw dogs translation in some form, and the latter two address it further in rather lengthy and helpful notes, as does Mitchell (also in his notes, though he does not use it in his translation).

Verse 7

☯ As mentioned, more traditional opening lines focus on various combinations of Heaven and Earth and take many forms. Some of them are included below:
  "Heaven is everlasting and Earth is ancient" (Beaulac);
  "Heaven is long and earth is lasting" (Mair 51);
  "Heaven and earth last forever" (Feng & English);
  "Heaven is long-enduring and earth continues long" (Legge);
  "Heaven is eternal, and Earth is long-lasting" (Mabry);
  "The universe is deathless" (Bynner);
  "The Tao is infinite, eternal" (Mitchell).

☯ Following up on the reference to Mitchell's quote in the comments: Another reference Joseph Campbell often made was to material from Neihardt's book *Black Elk Speaks*. Neihardt is telling of Black Elk's original early visions and notes one in which "Black Elk said the 'center of the world' mountain he stood upon in his vision was Harney Peak in the Black Hills. 'But anywhere is the center of the world,' he added."[2]

Campbell always marveled at the last comment, and usually compared it to the widely attributed[3] "God is an intelligible sphere whose center is everywhere and circumference nowhere." (A quote which, as you can imagine, also appeals to this old math type.)

Verse 8

I confess it was too many readings before I began to make connections between the first and second halves (or stanzas, depending on your translations) of this verse. Martin 2 (one of the verse choices) hands us one on a silver platter. He inserts "Were we to live this way" and forces us to notice a connection. But I've also become intrigued by Mitchell's translation (not included), where the connection isn't quite as obvious (and may be in my mind only?). His first stanza speaks of "water, which nourishes all things without trying to." Lately, the more I read the second stanza, the *feeling* is that were we to follow the suggestions there, we would be more open to—that is *sense*—this nourishment of that "supreme good." Even if that specific connection is unintended (by either Mitchell or Lao Tzu), it is helpful to me.

Verse 9

Martin has an excellent commentary on "a path of letting go" in his first section, "The Path" (p. 16).

Verse 10

☻ Besides other good notes in both Beaulac and Feng & English, there are also *abundant* notes on this verse in both Mitchell and in Mair (54, 113–114) (over a full page in the latter!).

☻ The last line of the verse ("the virtue of mystery" in Mabry) is also translated as follows:

"the supreme virtue" (Mitchell);
"true virtue" (Beaulac); and
"the Primal Virtue" (Feng & English).

Verse 12

☻ For excellent background notes on the five colors, tones, and tastes, see Beaulac and Mair (56.1, 56.7, 56.9; 114), among others.

☻ As mentioned in the comments, Martin's thrust of this verse is expressed in his "Outer things exist, but do not define us." Mitchell's rendition (not included) focuses on trusting the wisdom of our "inner vision" *vis-à-vis* the five senses. Similar sentiments, but just enough different to be enlightening, I think. Taken together they make a nice commentary.

Verse 13

☻ It's certainly not unusual for particular phrases to have a number of different translations. In this case, the extreme variety is most interesting to me. Here are some translations of the opening lines:

"Success is as dangerous as failure. / Hope is as hollow as fear" (Mitchell).

"'Favor and disgrace: both are sources of anxiety.' / 'Regard great affliction as a bodily matter'" (Beaulac).

"Success is often as unsettling as failure. / The world's troubles are no more important / than the well-being of your own body" (Mabry).

"Accept disgrace willingly. / Accept misfortune as the human condition" (Feng & English).

"'Being favored is so disgraceful that it startles, / Being honored is an affliction as great as one's body'" (Mair 57).

"Favour and disgrace would seem equally to be feared; honour and great calamity, to be regarded as personal conditions (of the same kind)" (Legge).

"Favor and disgrace have been called equal worries, / Success and failure have been called equal ailments" (Bynner).

"Winning can be just as bad as losing. / Confidence can mess you up just as much as fear" (Hogan).

"Favor and disgrace are equally dangerous; / honor and great calamity present the same challenges" (Breed).

☯ While realizing the two questions leading to explanations in this verse are rhetorical in nature, here are my own phrasings of the answers (as asked by Mitchell): "Success is as dangerous as failure" *because both have the ability to affect our ego and to distract from both our ego and our inner equilibrium.* "Hope is as hollow as fear" *because both exist in our minds only.*

Verse 16
The mentioned Einstein quote which Mitchell includes in his notes for this verse is as follows:

> The scientist's religious feeling takes the form of a rapturous amazement at the harmony of natural law, which reveals an intelligence of such superiority that, in comparison with it, all the systematic thinking of human beings is an utterly insignificant reflection. This feeling is the guiding principle of his life and work.

Verse 21
There are good notes for this verse in Beaulac and Feng & English.

Verse 23
Needleman's "most puzzling" sentence mentioned in the comments concludes with, "so much so that Richard Wilhelm writes 'On the whole, it is probably sensible to give up the passage as hopelessly beyond interpretation'" (Needleman [F&E], p. 94). I had to grin at that.

Verse 27
☯ I find the good person/bad person references—here, and in some other verses— puzzling, as the Tao Te Ching generally warns against over-naming and/or

labeling. If I were ever to undertake a translation (somewhere around the 12th of Never!), I would probably phrase those as "people who the world sees as good/bad" or something similar. Then again, I suspect that is *exactly* what Lao Tzu means, and Chinese language had no equivalent of quotation marks available to him.

☻ The last line of the 2nd stanza ("embodying the light" in Mitchell) is also translated in the following ways:
    "following one's light" (Beaulac);
    "following the light" (Feng & English);
    "inner intelligence" (Mair 71); and
    "Hiding the light of his procedure" (Legge).

☻ The last line of the verse ("the great secret" in both Mitchell and Martin) is also translated as follows:
    "the crux of mystery" (Feng & English);
    "seeing through to the essence" (Beaulac);
    "the wondrous essential" (Mair 71); and
    "The utmost degree of mystery" (Legge).

Verse 28
☻ Feng & English's translation gives a particularly good wording to stanzas 1 and 3, especially.

☻ Beaulac and Mair (72.27, 117) each have helpful notes.

☻ Martin's translation makes an insightful distinction between our struggles to create forms and functions and our ability to use them to the benefit of all.

Verse 32
Needleman (F&E) has an interesting (combined) note on both verses 32 and 34, commenting on the use of the word *small* in them.

Verse 33
☻ Bynner has a very nice rhyming version of this verse.

☻ Needleman (F&E), Martin 2, and Mair (77.8, 118) also provide insightful notes on this verse.

Verse 34
☻ See comment for verse 32 above.

☻ As Mitchell comments further on his own translation (included), he says that the Tao "acts without any conscious plan or purpose." So it certainly sounds like he would answer my "Is the Tao conscious?" question in the negative. And I might be hard-pressed to disagree myself. Perhaps, in the end, these thoughts boil down to a fascinating question in semantics. After all, I think "the Universe" is typically viewed (unconsciously?) as not having a consciousness, while I suspect "God" is almost universally viewed as conscious. And I don't think it's too much of a stretch to believe that the terms *Tao, Universe,* and *God*—while seldom used interchangeably, except by an occasional Taoist?—certainly tend, by their users anyway, to point in the same general direction.

Verse 36
Mabry's line, "Seeing this is an understanding of the subtle," is also translated in these ways:
>   "the subtle perception of the way things are" (Mitchell);
>   "obscure wisdom" (Beaulac);
>   "subtle insight" (Mair 80);
>   "Hiding the light" (Legge); and
>   "perception of the nature of things" (Feng & English).

Verse 39
A lengthy and excellent note in Beaulac provides insights on several parts of this verse, including some translating options and dilemmas, which in turn help account for some of the markedly different translations (Mair 2, e.g., and others).

Verse 42
Beaulac's note includes more thoughts on the one, two, and three in the first lines of the verse. Helpful notes on this verse also exist in Feng & English, Mitchell, and Mair (5.5–6 and 5.7; 108).

Verse 45
Concerning the "Old Boy" reference: Very early on, this reference to Lao Tzu was apparently not uncommon and was used in an affectionate and respectful way. (This is perhaps partly due to the very uncertainty of his actual existence as a historical figure.) This was one of two or three times that this moniker—or something similar—just felt appropriate to me and is used in that affectionate manner.

Verse 47
Concerning the *knowing the whole cosmos* and my mention of "not one, not two": I've heard or read this parable/fable in countless versions, and the message has become quite meaningful to me. Here is my own adaptation of the story.

There was a spiritual pilgrim who happened to encounter a Holy
Man. As Holy Men often do, he asked the pilgrim, "Do you have a
question?"

The pilgrim paused for a moment, and then said, "Well, yes. Yes, I do,
come to think of it. My question is: *Are God and I one?*"

The Holy Man smiled and lovingly replied, "Not one. Not two."

The pilgrim stared and said, "How can that be? I'm not sure that helps."

The Holy Man continued, "Consider this: The bird and its song, the sun
and its light, the dancer and the dance. Not one, but not two. Not the
same, but not different. So, you and God? Not one, not two.

The pilgrim slowly nodded, then smiled broadly. She turned and
resumed her pilgrimage, with a lighter step and an increased awareness
of God within her.

Verse 51

The subject of the last line of the verse ("Primal Virtue" in Feng & English) is also
translated in the following ways:
   "mystery of the Tao" (Breed);
   "Deep Virtue" (Beaulac);
   "mysterious integrity" (Mair 14); and
   "mysterious operation" (Legge).

Verse 52

The focus of the last line of the verse ("practicing consistency" in Mabry) is also
translated as follows:
   "practicing eternity" (Mitchell);
   "following the Eternal" (Beaulac); and
   "following the constant" (Mair 15).

Verse 53

Here is a fun (and enlightening) example which highlights the scholarly flavor to
Mair's notes: His translation's last stanza (Mair 16) reads "This is called 'the
brazenness of a bandit.' The brazenness of a bandit is surely not the Way!" In his
notes (16.15, 109), he mentions "There is an obvious pun here between 'bandit'
(*tao*) and 'the Way' (*Tao*). For similar reasons the thief is mentioned in the
Bhagavad Gita, III.12."

Verse 55
Neither quote in the last comment has a fixed wording. The first ("Too bad that
youth . . .") seems to be mostly, but not universally, associated with George
Bernard Shaw. The second ("Man does not . . .") can be found most often attached
to either Shaw or Oliver Wendell Holmes.

Verse 56
Note the similarity in the wordings in mid-verse to those of verse 52. Mair (19.4,
19.4–6, and 15.9; 108–109) has helpful comments on these wordings in his notes.

Verse 59
☯ Needleman (F&E) has one of his excellent notes for this verse, and Mair's
(relatively academic) note (22.2, 4; 109) discusses his early use of the word
"thrift" for the usual "moderation."

☯ Mabry's line "deep roots and a firm stalk" is also translated using these
phrases:
 "deep roots and a strong stem" (Mitchell, notes);
 "deep roots and a sturdy trunk" (Beaulac);
 "sinking roots firm and deep" (Mair 22);
 "roots are deep and its flower stalks firm" (Legge);
 "deep roots and a firm foundation" (Feng & English); and
 "deeply rooted plant with a sturdy stalk" (Breed).

Verse 62
Further thoughts on the second stanza, or its equivalent, depending on the
translation. As an example (and to dovetail on the thoughts in the comments),
Mitchell translates that stanza as follows:

> Honors can be bought with fine words,
> respect can be won with good deeds;
> but the Tao is beyond all value,
> and no one can achieve it.

With the usual variations, most translations have lines paralleling the first two
above. After that, things differ wildly—almost amusingly so. There appears to be
much confusion and uncertainty among translators about what the first two lines
are leading up to (and, for that matter, if/how they fit into the entire verse).

In the verse's comments, I focused on Mitchell's last line above, somewhat in
isolation, and suggested that the Tao is not something that can be *achieved* since it
is always around/with us. I now suspect that may be exactly Mitchell's
(interpretation of Lao Tzu's) point and that his translation has nailed it. *Honors*

and *respect* (and the other synonyms) can, in fact, be *won/bought/achieved*, whereas the Tao, being beyond value and of an entirely different nature, **cannot** be *achieved.* It is already part of us (and vice versa). This interpretation also seems to provide a more cohesive fit with the rest of the verse, I think.

Verse 65
The focus of the line, "This is called deep virtue!" in Beaulac is also translated in these ways:
"mystic virtue" (Breed);
"spiritual virtue" (Mabry);
"mysterious integrity" (Mair 28); and
"Primal Virtue" (Feng & English).

Verse 67
So many variations (including order) for the "three treasures"! Fasten your seat belt.
Mitchell: simplicity, patience, compassion.
Mitchell's (more traditional) note: compassion, frugality, and daring not to be first in the world.
Martin: compassion, simplicity, patience.
Mair (32): compassion, frugality, and not daring to be ahead of all under heaven.
Breed: gentleness, simplicity, humility.
Hogan: compassion, moderation, modesty.
Mabry: compassion, moderation, daring not to compete.
Legge: gentleness, economy, shrinking from taking precedence of others.
Beaulac: compassion, frugality, and reluctance to put myself first in the world.
Bynner: to care, to be fair, to be humble.
Feng & English: mercy, economy, daring not to be ahead of others.

Verse 68
The line of the verse translated as "Virtue of not striving" in Feng & English is also translated in these ways:
"*te* of not competing" (Mitchell, notes);
"virtue of non-aggression" (Beaulac); and
"integrity without competition," (Mair 33).

Verse 73
The story that follows (verse 74) seems to apply to this verse as well.

Verse 74

There are numerous versions of the mentioned parable/folk tale. Mitchell quotes one he says comes from the *Huai Nan Tzu*. The following (shorter) version comes from the website of The Philosophy Man, Ltd.:

> This is the story of an old Chinese farmer who lived many years ago.
> He had one old horse that he used to plough his fields.
>
> One day, the horse ran away into the hills.
> Everyone said, "We are so sorry for your bad luck."
> The old man replied, "Bad luck, good luck, who knows?"
>
> A week later, the horse returned with a herd of wild horses, which now belonged to the old man.
> Everyone said, "We are so happy for your good luck!"
> The old man replied, "Good luck, bad luck, who knows?"
>
> While his only son was riding one of the wild horses, he fell off and broke his leg.
> Everyone said, "What bad luck!"
> The old man replied, "Bad luck, good luck, who knows?"
>
> One day, the army came to the village, and took all the strong young men to be soldiers for the emperor. Only the old farmer's son was spared because he could not fight with a broken leg.
> Everyone said, "What good luck!"
> The old man replied, "Good luck, bad luck, who knows?"[4]

(Other versions continue on with further events in a similar manner.)

Verse 81

The remainder of the verse ends with a by-now familiar theme of simplicity in living, usually with some kind of a warning about collecting—even hoarding—possessions. Mitchell's version translates it as "The Master has no possessions." But I've always been both amused and struck by his later comment: "These no-possessions may include a house, a car, a computer, a roomful of books, and an electric toothbrush." Perhaps this will seem to be stretching things, but I think the insight behind the humor points to the subtle difference between possessing things and having things that *possess* the owner. I think the simplicity of Tao speaks less about possessions themselves than our attachment to them and/or the distraction they may cause on our journeys. I'm reminded of the rich, young ruler in the gospels who could not give away his wealth and "went away [from Jesus] sorrowful, for he had great possessions" (Matthew 19:22, English Standard Version). I'm also reminded how difficult such non-attachment is to achieve!

176

Notes

1. Joseph Campbell, *Pathways to Bliss: Mythology and Personal Transformation* (Novato, CA: New World Library, 2004), 112.

2. John G. Neihardt, *Black Elk Speaks: Being the Life Story of a Holy Man of the Oglala Sioux as Told through John G. Neihardt (Flaming Rainbow)* (University of Nebraska Press, 1993), 42–43.
    I share this at the risk of getting too far afield, but in pinning down some of these facts again, I discovered a blog called Mesocosm (also written by Mesocosm, its address is https://mesocosm.net/2012/12/11/black-elk/), which, on the surface, makes a believable case that Neihardt embellished much of the information about and quotes from Black Elk. I found this fascinating but only mention it as an aside since I have no way of knowing the truth here.

3. I have seen this (or interesting-but-highly-similar versions) attributed to everyone from early Greek philosophy (Hermeticism, in particular) to Voltaire, Pascal, and many others in between.

4. Jason Buckley, The Philosophy Man (website), accessed October 9, 2021, https://www.thephilosophyman.com/wp-content/uploads/2012/01/Good-Luck -Bad-Luck-Enquiry-Plan.pdf.

References

Beaulac, Andrew. 2016. *Sitting with Lao Tzu*. Berkeley, CA: Apocryphile Press.

Breed, George. 2014. *Jesus and Lao Tzu: Adventures with the Tao Te Ching*. Vestal, NY: Anamchara Books.

Bynner, Witter. 1986. *The Way of Life According to Lao Tzu*. New York: A Perigee Book published by the Berkley Publishing Group, a division of Penguin Putnam, Inc.

Chen, Ellen. 1989. *The Tao Te Ching: A New Translation with Commentary*. St. Paul, MN: Paragon House.

Cohen, Alan. 2018. *The Tao Made Easy*. Carlsbad, CA: Hay House, Inc.

Hogan, Ron. 2010. *Getting Right with Tao: A Contemporary Spin on the Tao Te Ching*. New York: Channel V Books, a division of Channel V Media.

Mabry, John R. 1994. *Tao Te Ching: The Book of the Way and Its Power*. Berkeley, CA: Apocryphile Press.

Martin, William. 2005. *A Path and a Practice*. New York: Marlowe & Company, an imprint of Avalon Publishing Group, Inc.

Martin, William. 2016. *Walking the Tao*. Mount Shasta, CA: Taoist Living.

Mitchell, Stephen. 2006. *Tao Te Ching: A New English Version*, Harper Perennial Modern Classics edition. New York: HarperCollins Publishers.

Mitchell, Stephen. 2009. *The Second Book of the Tao*. New York: The Penguin Press, published by the Penguin Group.

Pine, Red, translator. 1996. *Lao-tzu's Taoteching*. San Francisco, CA: Mercury House.

Tsu, Lao. 1989. *Tao Te Ching*. Translated by Gia-fu Feng and Jane English. Introduction and notes by Jacob Needleman. New York: Vintage Books, a division of Random House, Inc.

Tzu, Lao. 1990. *TAO TE CHING*. Translated and annotated by Victor H. Mair. New York: Bantam Books.

Tzu, Lao. 2016. *Tao Te Ching*. Translated with commentary by James Legge. N.p.: Digireads.com Publishing.

Author Index

Each of the authors whose translations are used in this book is listed below, along with the number of each of the verses where their translations may be found.

Beaulac
2, 8, 9, 12, 13, 14, 16, 21, 22, 24, 26, 27, 32, 33, 35, 38, 39, 40, 41, 42, 47, 52, 56, 57, 58, 59, 63, 64, 65, 71, 73, 74, 75, 76, 77, 78, 80

Breed
6, 18, 25, 26, 31, 37, 51, 54, 56, 60, 61, 66, 67, 68, 81

Bynner
2, 3, 12, 15, 36, 42, 46, 47, 50, 67, 70, 74

Feng & English
3, 24, 29, 31, 43, 44, 46, 51, 53, 68, 72, 73

Hogan
4, 5, 7, 15, 20, 23, 30, 33, 41, 48, 50, 53, 57, 62, 66, 78, 80

Legge
6, 11, 19, 55, 61, 63, 75, 77, 79

Mabry
3, 4, 5, 8, 10, 11, 16, 18, 20, 21, 28, 31, 32, 34, 35, 36, 37, 40, 43, 44, 46, 48, 49, 52, 56, 59, 61, 62, 63, 64, 65, 69, 70, 75, 81

Mair
1, 9, 14, 17, 45, 49, 60, 66, 71, 76, 79

Martin
1, 7, 9, 11, 12, 15, 16, 17, 18, 19, 20, 22, 24, 27, 29, 32, 39, 40, 42, 47, 49, 54, 57, 59, 62, 67, 68, 69, 70, 72, 76, 77, 78

Martin 2
2, 4, 5, 6, 8, 10, 13, 14, 21, 23, 25, 26, 28, 30, 33, 34, 35, 36, 37, 38, 41, 43, 44, 45, 48, 50, 51, 52, 53, 55, 58, 60, 64, 71, 73, 79, 80, 81

Mitchell
1, 7, 10, 13, 17, 19, 22, 23, 25, 27, 28, 29, 30, 34, 38, 39, 45, 54, 55, 58, 65, 69, 72, 74

One-Word Title Index

A list of some one-word descriptions of the various verses (see "A Dozen Loose Ends" in the introduction). Verse titles are indicated in all uppercase, with secondary themes capitalized normally.

Abundance: 4, 5
ACCEPTANCE: 22
Acceptance: 36
ACCORD: 60
Appearances: 41, 58, 73
Attachment: 44
ATTENTION: 63
AUTHENTIC: 18
Authentic: 20
Awareness: 53, 63
AWE: 72
BALANCE: 77
Balance: 2, 24, 39
BEGINNINGS: 64
Benefit: 28
CENTERED: 19
Centered: 5, 13, 16, 26, 29, 77
Content: 10, 46
CONTENTMENT: 44
Contentment: 3, 33, 79, 80
Contradictions: 41
CONTROL: 74
Control: 29
Death: 50
Dedication: 53
Deep: 25
Desire: 1
Detached: 7
Detachment: 16, 47, 50
DISTINCTIONS: 32
Distractions: 12
DUALITY: 2
Duality: 42
Eden: 80
Effortless: 37, 43
EMPOWERING: 75
Emptiness: 11

Encompassing: 32
ENEMIES: 69
Enlightenment: 15
ENOUGH: 46
Enough: 30, 44
Essence: 27
ETERNAL: 7
Eternal: 21
EXAMPLE: 58
EXCESS: 24
EXPRESSION: 51
Feminine: 6
Flexibility: 36
FLEXIBLE: 76
Flexible: 49
FLOW: 29
Flow: 8, 23, 43, 45
Focus: 53
FREE: 20
Gentle: 78
Genuine: 18, 58
Greatness: 34, 61
GROUNDED: 26
HARMONY: 39
Harmony: 17, 42, 55
Here: 47
HUMILITY: 66
Humility: 39, 61
Hypocrisy: 18
IDEAL: 80
IMPARTIAL: 5
INEXHAUSTIBLE: 35
Infinite: 7
INNER: 47
Inner: 12
INTANGIBLE: 11
INTEGRITY: 79

Integrity: 38
INTERNAL: 12
INVALUABLE: 62
Invisible: 14
Joy: 57
LAUGHABLE: 41
LEADERSHIP: 17
Leadership: 57, 66
LIFE: 50
Life: 75
LIVING: 57
Living: 8
MASTERY: 48
MIND: 71
Mindful: 15
MODERATION: 59
MOTHER: 6
Mother: 25
MYSTERY: 14
Mystery: 21, 25, 72
Nameless: 32
NATURAL: 23
Nature: 10, 18, 19
NET: 73
NON-ACTION: 43
NON-AGGRESSION: 68
Non-being: 11
Non-competition: 68
Non-contention: 81
Non-interference: 48, 57, 60
NON-KNOWING: 65
Non-knowing: 71
NOURISHING: 81
Nourishment: 8
Omnipotent: 37
OMNIPRESENT: 34
Omnipresent: 62
One: 47
ONENESS: 10
Oneness: 13, 56
OPEN: 27
Open: 12, 23, 49
ORIGIN: 21

Origin: 52
ORIGINS: 4
OVERDOING: 30
Overdoing: 9
Overreach: 24
PARADOXICAL: 78
Path: 70
Passive: 6
PEACE: 31
Peace: 35
PERCEPTION: 36
PERFECTION: 45
Perfection: 22
PERSPECTIVE: 13
Perspective: 23, 44
Present: 15, 50
Punishment: 74
Purity: 58
Quietness: 40
RECEPTIVE: 28
RELEASE: 9
Release: 10, 22, 36
Resistance: 30
Responsibility: 79
Restraint: 30
Results: 42
RETURN: 40
ROOTED: 54
Safety: 35
SAGE: 15
SENSES: 52
Separateness: 13
Service: 28
SIDETRACKED: 53
Silent: 56
Simple: 48
SIMPLICITY: 37
Simplicity: 3, 80
Soft: 78
Softness: 76
Source: 62
Steadfast: 54
STILLNESS: 16

Strength: 35
Sufficient: 33
SUSTENANCE: 8
TAO: 25
Tranquility: 16
TRANSPARENT: 49
TREASURES: 67
Trinity: 67
Trio: 67
Trust: 59
Unattached: 81
UNDERSTANDING: 70
Undisturbed: 20
Ungraspable: 14
UNION: 56
Unity: 21, 40

Universality: 73
Unknowns: 73
VIRTUE: 38
Virtues: 67
VITALITY: 55
Watcher: 7
WAY: 1
Way: 38, 70
Wholeness: 22, 38
WISDOM: 33
Wisdom: 3, 29, 60, 71, 81
WU-WEI: 3
Wu-Wei: 9, 43, 45, 48
YIELDING: 61
Yielding: 76, 78
YIN-YANG: 42

Other Translations

There are *dozens* of English translations of the Tao Te Ching, not surprising since, after the Bible, it is the most translated book in the world. (See below for a link to many more.) So, I should stress that the collection of eleven translations included in this book, as well as those mentioned in this section, are not intended to form an exhaustive (or even extensive) list, nor are they intended to imply any level of objective excellence above any other translations not mentioned. I would encourage you to seek your own favorites. (I would also be delighted to hear of any personal gems that *you* discover. See Contacting the Author.)

Having said that, here are a half dozen more translations that I will briefly single out here, with some further notes about each. I have used most of these at least once in my own quarterly readings.

Walker (*The Tao Te Ching of Lao Tzo* by Brian Browne Walker. St. Martin's Essentials, an imprint of St. Martin's Publishing Group, 1995.)
This book is *very high* on my list of frequently used favorites. I had wanted (and planned) to feature a large number of his translations, but alas . . . Macmillan had other plans. If/when you are in the market for a(nother) translation choice, I recommend you take a good look at this book. Other than a short preface, there are no other notes or background material, but his translations and wordings are, quite often, *so* good.

Red Pine (*Lao-tzu's Taoteching* translated by Red Pine (Bill Porter). Mercury House, 1996.)
This is another book I had originally planned to include, but it also fell victim to various glitches in and ramifications of the permission processes. Its inclusion would have made it a nice companion for Mair as the most scholarly of the renditions. The book has several recommending features beyond its translations, at least two of which are quite rare: (1) alongside his (English) translation of each verse, he also places the Chinese version of the verse; and (2) each verse is accompanied by *several* quotes about parts of the verse from a variety of Chinese scholars, both (presumably) past and more recent. Further, his introductory matter is quite good, and he includes an interesting glossary in the back.

Chen (*The Tao Te Ching: A New Translation with Commentary* by Ellen Chen. Paragon House, 1989.)
This translation was hiding in my collection of lesser-used translations, as I had not planned to include it in the collection of translations used. But I was later pleased to discover what an incredible set of notes and background material it has! Each verse is followed by *both* a general comment of a few sentences *and* a quite lengthy and detailed comment (with emphasis on the detailed!). A small number of the insights from her general comments are quoted (and referenced) in the

comments here, and these may entice you to explore the book further. Usually, each of those contains helpful and enlightening material. On top of that, the book opens with a 50-page introduction containing an amazing amount of background material. After the translation, both a glossary and an index also appear.

Pepper & Wang (*Dao De Jing in Clear English*, translation and commentary by Jeff Pepper and Xiao Hui Wang. Imagin8 Press, 2018.)
Like Red Pine, Pepper & Wang include a Chinese translation, but it's a line-by-line breakdown of the Chinese with added features. Each verse starts with an entire (English) translation. Following that is a fascinating section consisting of 4 parts for *each* line or grouping: (1) a repeat of the English line; (2) the Chinese version of that line, coupled with an English rendition of each symbol; (3) the English translation of the literal sentence of Chinese symbols; and (4) a brief comment. The book has the potential to be an amazing resource, especially for the more serious seeker/student looking for more specialized translation details.

Lin (*Tao Te Ching: Annotated & Explained*, translation and annotation by Derek Lin. Skylights Paths Publishing, 2006.)
I probably used this book three or four times in my early readings but have drifted away from it lately. The book has a helpful set of introductory material and an interesting list of suggestions for further reading in the back. There are notes accompanying each verse, conveniently placed on the facing page, with footnote-style referencing.

Cleary (*The Essential Tao: An Initiation into the Heart of Taoism through the Authentic* Tao Te Ching *and the Inner Teachings of* Chuang-Tzu, translated and presented by Thomas Cleary. HarperCollins Paperback edition, HarperSanFrancisco, a division of HarperCollins Publishers, 1993.)
This book is over 30 years old but has a good following and is considered a classic by some. The individual translations themselves did not often speak *to me*, but there is an incredible wealth of other material in the book, including a translation of Chuang-tzu (another ancient Chinese classic) that follows the translation of the Tao Te Ching. The introduction is a good one (and I have underlined often in it). At the end, there is a lengthy section of historical background of Taoism, the Tao Te Ching, and Chuang-tzu, as well as a separate set of notes for *each* translation. It is a valuable resource, as well as reference.

****

For an extensive list of English Tao Te Ching translations available see https://terebess.hu/english/tao/_index.html. It should be noted, however, that this list is apparently not exhaustive (as I don't see at least four of the translations used here, e.g.!). It also has links to bare-bones verse translations for most, if not all, volumes, but no other ancillary information is included.

188

Further Suggested Reading

Over the years, I have developed a collection of books I like (and use) which are related to the material in the Tao Te Ching. I suspect some of you have also developed such a collection. I'd be delighted to share my list, and I'd like to allow you to share yours—if you wish—making it a dynamic, ongoing list, as we regularly find new ones we like as well. Hopefully, this could be a good resource for us.

As this book prepares to "go to press," this list, its addition to my website, *and* the updating to that website are all in progress, but should be finished shortly after the book's publication, if not before. Feel free to visit that site (www.larryncampbell.com) and you should be able to find the list under the MY BOOKS tab. (If you have trouble, contact me—see below—and I'll send you a link.)

Contacting the Author

The author would be happy to hear from you for any of the following reasons:
- Discuss any topics in this book, share related insights on the content, and/or discoveries of unmentioned translations or other sharings.
- Submit a review of the book for possible inclusion on the website (or a later edition of the book).
- Add/suggest a book for Further Readings (see Further Readings above).
- Order inscribed copies of any of his books (inscribing/signing is free) or inquire about current special discounts.
- Make suggestions concerning the author's website, future editions of the book, or something else. (If the author uses your suggestion(s), he will double the amount he's left you in his will.)
- Ask to be kept updated on new developments related to the author's books, presentations, podcasts, and/or other activities.
- Sign up for his (free—and fun) Bi-Weekly Mailings. (Want to do this now? Go to https://larrycampbell.com/index.php/contact.)
- Schedule (or inquire about) a Zoom or on-site presentation.
- *Almost* any other (legal) reason.

To contact the author, you may either visit his website (larryncampbell.com) and use the Contact Form there (also listed above) or e-mail him directly at larrycampbell@aftermathenterprises.com.

Other Books by the Author

Rollin' Down the River: Discovering People and Places Along the Mighty Missouri (Acclaim Press, 2017)

"The Adventure of a Lifetime," this coffee table book details the author's 2016 seven-week journey, following the Missouri River (by car) from its source in Three Forks, MT, to where it ends near St. Louis, MO. With over 200 of the author's pictures, and many narratives of the trip's itinerary, cities, adventures, and marvelous residents, the book will take you on your own adventure from the comfort of your home!

Spitballs from the Back Row: Essays on the Modern American Education System (Oghma Creative Media, 2018)

MORE Spitballs from the Back Row: Another Collection of Essays on the Modern American Education System (2020)

How do you define "a good education"? What does it mean to be *educated?* Public education has long been an incredibly complex venture, and—two decades into the 21st century, in an increasingly technological age and politically divided society— it certainly is not getting any easier. In these collections of previously published newspaper columns, the author brings a variety of educational issues to the surface, raises subtle and different perspectives, minimizes misperceptions, and provides balance, always in a light, readable, and occasionally humorous style.

Praise for the Author and His Books

ROLLIN' DOWN THE RIVER: Discovering People and Places Along the Mighty Missouri

"With a mathematician's attention to detail, an adventurer's insatiable curiosity and his own unassuming, friendly and open way of meeting the world, Larry Campbell is the perfect person for a journey like this. Let yourself settle in and enjoy this information-packed and yet lighthearted exploration of the Missouri River and her people."

Gayle Harper, Travel Photographer and Writer;
Author of *Roadtrip with a Raindrop: 90 Days Along the Mississippi*

"[What a] good story-teller . . . everything flows like the Missouri River on a Summer day . . . Grab this book, a comfortable chair, and a drink of your choice and become an Armchair Traveler."

Beverly Hinds, President
The Middle Missouri River Lewis and Clark Network

"What's not to like about a colorful and entertaining recount of an incredible adventure that I honestly wish I had thought to undertake! From castles and cathedrals in remote locales to . . . kind locals who opened their world to Campbell, the vignettes are lively and poignant. A comfortable story telling style ties together the power and glory of nature with the hope of human beings."

Todd Parnell, Author of *The Buffalo, Ben, and Me* (and others);
Past President, Drury College in Springfield, MO

"The beautiful photography and descriptive passages . . . added to the local color and kept my interest . . . as I read [them], I felt like I had been right there with him. Campbell did much more than just tell the history of the 'Mighty Mo.' He actually took me with him on his adventure."

Sunny Hannum, Fort Pierre (SD) Development Corporation

SPITBALLS FROM THE BACK ROW and *MORE Spitballs from the Back Row*

"[Campbell is] a latter-day Mark Twain!"

"Skip" Fennell, Past President of National Council of
Teachers of Mathematics. (From the *Spitballs* Foreword)

"Dr. Campbell has the wonderful knack of bringing a new viewpoint on . . . topics and of influencing the reader to consider other perspectives."

Shirley M. Frye, Past President, National Council of Teachers of Mathematics

"Dr. Campbell approaches the challenges facing education in the twenty-first century in a very thoughtful and engaging manner . . . an unusual ability to see the interesting in the midst of the mundane."

Dr. David Sallee, President Emeritus, William Jewell College

"Worthy of your time if you care at all about our future."

Peter Herschend, Past President, Missouri State School Board

About the Author

Dr. Larry Campbell spent most of his professional career working as a professor in mathematics and mathematics education, split equally (17 years each) between the College of the Ozarks near Branson, MO, and Missouri State University in Springfield, MO. Between those stops, he also spent three years as President of Ozark Mountain Community Classroom in Branson.

He retired from Missouri State—in stages—between 2010 and 2012, and since then, he has been running AfterMath Enterprises, LLC, an umbrella organization for all the activities in which he is engaged. Besides doing (in non-pandemic times) a variety of presentations, programs, and workshops for civic/community groups and schools, he also puts out a (free) bi-weekly photo/sharing e-mail blog which combines his photography hobby with several other Monday morning brighteners and tidbits for the week, and has regularly written a bi-weekly education column for the *Springfield [MO] News-Leader*.

Larry and his wife, Pat, live in Branson, MO. They have two grown children, Christi and Adam.